# PROMISSORY NOTES

# Promissory Notes

ON THE
LITERARY CONDITIONS
OF DEBT

By Robin Truth Goodman
*Professor and Associate Chair of English*
*Florida State University*

LEVER
PRESS

Lever Press (leverpress.org) is a publisher of pathbreaking scholarship. Supported by a consortium of liberal arts institutions focused on, and renowned for, excellence in both research and teaching, our press is grounded on three essential commitments: to be a digitally native press, to be a peer-reviewed, open access press that charges no fees to either authors or their institutions, and to be a press aligned with the ethos and mission of liberal arts colleges.

The proposal of this work was subjected to a fully closed ("double blind") review process. The complete manuscript of this work was subjected to a partly closed ("single blind") review process. For more information, please see our Peer Review Commitments and Guidelines at https://www.leverpress.org/peerreview

DOI: https://doi.org/10.3998/mpub.10209707
Print ISBN: 978-1-64315-000-0
Open access ISBN: 978-1-64315-002-7

LCCN: 2018958665

Published in the United States of America by Lever Press, in partnership with Amherst College Press and Michigan Publishing
Manufactured in the United States of America

You no longer need foreign armies to control the population . . . [Debt] has rendered historical concepts of national independence almost meaningless.

—Juan González

It is well enough that the people of the nation do not understand our banking and monetary system, for if they did, I believe that there would be a revolution before tomorrow morning.

—Henry Ford Sr.

*Acknowledgments*

Lever Press is a joint venture. This work was made possible by the generous support of Lever Press member libraries from the following institutions:

Adrian College
Agnes Scott College
Allegheny College
Amherst College
Bard College
Berea College
Bowdoin College
Carleton College
Claremont Graduate University
Claremont McKenna College
Clark Atlanta University
Coe College
College of Saint Benedict / Saint John's University
The College of Wooster
Denison University
DePauw University
Earlham College
Furman University
Grinnell College
Guilford College
Hamilton College
Harvey Mudd College
Haverford College
Hollins University
Interdenominational Theological Center
Keck Graduate Institute
Kenyon College
Knox College
Lafayette College
Lake Forest College
Macalester College

Middlebury College
Morehouse College
Oberlin College
Pitzer College
Pomona College
Rollins College
Santa Clara University
Scripps College
Sewanee: The University of the South
Skidmore College
Smith College
Spelman College
St. Lawrence University
St. Olaf College
Susquehanna University
Swarthmore College
Trinity University
Union College
University of Puget Sound
Ursinus College
Vassar College
Washington and Lee University
Whitman College
Williams College

## *Contents*



*Online Appendix: https://doi.org/10.3998/mpub.10209390.fulcrum.cmp.1*

# INTRODUCTION

"You know the old joke," begins David Dayen of *The Nation*. "How do you make a killing on Wall Street and never risk a loss? Easy—use other people's money" (13). Dayen's article is about J. P. Morgan's settlement on a case of misconduct when they "robo-signed" possibly thousands of foreclosures after the housing crisis of 2008. By "robo-signed," Dayen means that J. P. Morgan did not investigate the contents of the foreclosure documents. In a 2013 settlement, J. P. Morgan was required to forgive $4.2 billion worth of foreclosures and pay another $4 billion in consumer relief for deceiving mortgage investors. In order to comply with the settlement, however, J. P. Morgan "was forgiving loans *on properties it no longer owned*" (13; original emphasis). J. P. Morgan had sold tens of thousands of toxic loans years before at bargain rates in order to get the loans off its balance sheet (1st Fidelity Loan Services is the buyer that Dayen focuses on in a deal arranged by Nationwide Title Clearing, associated with, weirdly enough, the Church of Scientology) and yet had not taken the properties out of its secret "dump" of distressed properties and had not even provided full documentation on the properties to those who bought the loans, even admitting that they were still collecting payments on those properties.

They then proceeded to "forgive" the loans they no longer owned in order to honor the mortgage forgiveness requirements in the settlement. Dayen concludes that the Justice Department under the Trump administration is unlikely to pursue litigation.

The issue here is not only that bankers have been profiting from using other people's money by expanding debt. Dayen's story also shows that bankers have taken over the sovereign state's role of creating money by creating characters who hold the same money that they do at the same time as they do[1]—this made it possible for them to own the same money twice. In other words, the old joke really is that bankers are making money by using *nobody's money* or, rather, using *no thing* that still has the name of money in order to create more money for themselves under a different name. That is, bankers are profiting from using their own money multiple times by distributing the same money to multiple fictional entities with multiple fictional personalities under multiple fictional names: they are, in essence, sharing the profits from their properties with multiple versions of themselves. J. P. Morgan could then claim (e.g., if a payment came in) that they were the owners of the loans even while they could also claim (e.g., if there were an enforcement issue or an associated cost) that another company was responsible. The practice of expanding the money supply by expanding debt—that is, of expanding the money supply by representing money in multiple money endeavors at once—is not aberrant or criminal but quite simply the rule of capital.

J. P. Morgan was the company that came up with the idea of what is now broadly called the credit default swap (also known as "synthetic collateralized debt obligations" or "securitization"). The credit default swap is an instrument that furthered the excesses that most people believe led to the 2008 financial crisis. It basically allowed financial companies to reduce their reserves and transfer the risks of the loan to another company. According to British novelist John Lanchester in his nonfiction account of the crisis, *I.O.U.*, in 1989, Exxon needed to open up a credit line to fund cleanup after the *Exxon Valdez* spill. J. P. Morgan had a long-standing relationship with Exxon and wanted to help them out, but the money could be better spent elsewhere, since the cleanup was not likely to be lucrative. So J. P. Morgan came up with the idea of selling the loan to the European Bank for Reconstruction and Development for a fee. That way, J. P. Morgan did not need to hold reserves against the loan and could still use their reserves to loan out the same money to someone else, and the regulators looked the other way because the banks could say they were maintaining the legal level of reserves (remember, all this was to cover the costs of a sinking ship, so to speak). "J.P. Morgan," concludes Lanchester, "had found a way to shift risk off its books, while simultaneously generating income from that risk and freeing up capital to lend elsewhere" (70). This mechanism could succeed in a time of growth, but if money were receding, the banks could not pay because they were overleveraged.

Eventually, the third-party bank that held the loan was replaced by financial instruments that bundled up the loans, mixing different levels of risk assessed not by evaluating a person or company's financial records and histories[2] but rather through complex mathematical models that referred to constructed averages, composites, and bell curves rather than to actual financial actors. The bundles of loans absorbed risk by dispersing it throughout the system to a variety of named entities.[3]

These J. P. Morgan incidents divulge a trend in financial methods: that is, finance is indebted to literary practices. In this instance, profits are made by constructing believable characters who transact on a believable financial stage. They are made as characters by holding money, as their personalities are built on traditions of securing value that literature has developed as well as on literary traditions that envision characters as a composite of social positions and averages so that they seem compelling, identifiable, and sympathetic across a broad array of types of readers. Similar to the way J. P. Morgan created shells to hold value, for nineteenth-century novelists like Anthony Trollope, for example, mentioning the value of a person's assets and annual income did a lot of the work of establishing character traits, often stood in for explaining the character's moral positions, and also revealed the character's social networks and place in the community (in terms not only of class but also of influence, trustworthiness, political potential, and connections). "The revenues from the Scotch estate," *The Eustace Diamonds* narrator tells us about the recently widowed Lizzie Eustace, "—some £4000 a year—were clearly her own for life" (52), whereas her sometimes lover Frank Greystock, "at present . . . was almost nobody;—because he was so poor, and in debt" (255), and her one-time fiancé Lord Fawn "had declared to his future bride that he had half five thousand a year to spend" (114). Additionally, nineteenth-century writers like Trollope were interested in how new forms of property ownership, not based in land or objects but rather in finance, might require new types of narrative framing and characterization, which destabilized the "intrinsik value" in things (established in their price), just as J. P. Morgan was able to untether value from actual things by transferring that value onto an imaginary elsewhere: a bank or, later, a bundle of debts. In fact, what J. P. Morgan and Trollope share is a grappling with the question of the imaginary as necessary for constructing real value. *Promissory Notes* focuses on a historical relation between fiction and finance, where the line between them is blurry. In effect, it considers how financial instruments appropriate techniques of fiction and literary representation to build the representations of value that organize their systems.

There is no doubt that the beginning of the twenty-first century was marked by crises of debt. Student debt is the highest in history, reaching $1.3 trillion in 2017, according to Zack Friedman of *Forbes*. As Maurizio Lazzarato notes of US universities, "This temple for the transmission and production of Western knowledge is also a model of the financial institution, and, with it, of the debt economy . . . On the one hand, the American university is the ideal realization of the creditor-debtor relationship. On the other hand, the American student perfectly embodies the condition of the indebted man by serving as paradigm for the conditions of subjectivation of the debt economy one finds throughout society" (*Governing* 64). In addition, according to Jessica Silver-Greenberg and Stacy Cowley in the *New York Times*, outstanding credit card debt in 2017 reached its highest point in history at $1 trillion, with more Americans holding credit cards than ever before. Though Republicans (and many Democrats) have been campaigning against national deficit spending for decades, the tax reform bill they passed at the end of 2017 is predicted to raise the deficit by more than $1 trillion, according to the nonpartisan Congressional Budget Office (CBO), reaching record highs. Debt in neoliberalism underlies what Lazzarato identifies as "an asymmetrical class struggle" (*Governing* 12): "What is expropriated by credit/debt," he continues, "is not only wealth, knowledge, and the 'future,' but more fundamentally the possible" (*Governing* 23). Such national debts are paid for with austerity policies, cuts to safety nets and education, and cuts in wages and benefits. In an interview with Jeremy Scahill of *The Intercept*, geographer David Harvey has called these practices "debt peonage" and their enforcement "the militarization of social control, and the intense militarization and the super-militarization of it": "One of the ways in which social control is exercised," he asserts, "is to get people so deep in debt they cannot imagine anything in the future other than simply living in such a way as to pay off their debt."

Literature has played a historical role in defining and teaching debt to the public. Realism in the novel developed in the nineteenth century alongside the standardization of such monetary instruments as paper currency, coin, balance sheets, stocks, and credit bills and shared with credit culture the need to produce a belief in something that, by definition, *is not there*. For example, in Anthony Trollope's 1873 novel *The Eustace Diamonds*, the plot begins with a debt that takes the form of a necklace whose ownership and value cannot be traced. Much of the plot of *The Eustace Diamonds* focuses on how legal language unsuccessfully describes what objects such as the diamonds—like debt, of negative content—are within a property framework based in concrete materials. The loss of value in landed properties meant that the source of value, like meaning in language, came to seem shifty as value was increasingly transferred onto moveable objects or investment speculation such as the diamonds. In *The Eustace Diamonds*, nineteenth-century Britain witnesses a transition from an eighteenth-century idea of property, where value is intrinsic to the object, to an idea of property whose value is representational and whose representation can lie or prove empty, without reference. Dependent effectively on establishing connections between fiction and belief, literature adds credibility to finance: finance's elusiveness requires the types of speculative narrative, readers, predictable characters, and abstract social worlds developed in realist and postrealist forms. The nineteenth-century British realist novel was often a place where the effects of these changes on social relations could be considered, experimented with, and tested and where readers could be taught to believe.

Indeed, literary figuration is central to testing, teaching, and recognizing the political imposition of debt. Early twentieth-century literary writers recognized debt as a fiction wielded to extend imperial power and exposed such practices, creating a new awareness and somewhat of a backlash leading to new legislation, federal personnel changes, and even some criminal charges. In 1932, for example, the African American poet Langston Hughes wrote a newspaper polemic about the early twentieth-century crisis and military occupation of Haiti, explaining, "You will discover that the Banque d'Haiti, with its Negro cashiers and tellers is really under control of the National City Bank of New York. You will become informed that all the money collected by the Haitian customs passes through the hands of an American comptroller." With an even greater impact, in 1920, African American author and educator James Weldon Johnson wrote a four-part series of articles for *The Nation* in which he spotlighted the military invasion and occupation of Haiti as defending the interests of the National City Bank of New York, which controlled the ports, the treasury, the issuance of bonds, and the importation and exportation of currency. Leading into the third article, which recounts the history of the New York Bank taking over the Haitian public and private financial system, Johnson writes, "This Government forced the Haitian leaders to accept the promise of American aid and American supervision. With that American aid the Haitian Government defaulted its external and internal debt, an obligation, which under self-government the Haitians had scrupulously observed. And American supervision turned out to be a military tyranny supporting the program of economic exploitation" (38–39).

The practice continues. Just to mention a few titles published in the wake of the 2008 crisis, Jess Walter's 2009 novel *The Financial Lives of the Poets* tells of a financial reporter / poet who loses his newspaper job as well as his own blog site/start-up business (which he calls "money-lit" [48] because it uses poetry to explain finance) just when his house goes underwater. His cool, sardonic narrative voice—as well as his adventurous exploits, upon unemployment, as a pot dealer who eventually falls in with large suppliers and growers and then with the FBI as an informant—turns what should realistically be a tragic tale of national need and instability into a comedic jostle through drugged-up desperation and adorable failure. Martha McPhee's 2010 novel *Dear Money* features a formerly semisuccessful novelist who, when her house quite literally goes underwater ("Water from the storm that had draped Connecticut in glistening beauty on our return had penetrated the roof of our apartment building and dripped through the ceiling and onto, and then into, our mattress" [67]), is seduced by a bond trader who solicits her to work for his Wall Street firm. The novel has interspersed informational asides that explain from the future the development of shady financial instruments, often punctuated by the narrator's own cute naïveté as an outsider to the industry, like this one: "Most of all the idea of pooling people, of trying to understand how they operated psychologically . . . as a collective lot . . . was better than the plot of any story I'd read in a while . . . This was imagination at work, imagination with consequences—nothing less" (48).

Some postcolonial literature has also taken on narratives of debt, teasing out the conventions of imaginative writing embedded in the social relations of debt emerging in postcolonial space and evolving into neoliberal globalization. Indeed, *The Eustace Diamonds* compares the diamonds to the status of India in a subplot about the legitimacy of its principality after the 1857 Indian Mutiny. As with the diamonds and debt, such a formulation of colonized space as particularly exploitable due to its alienated, fictional, or negative status in relation to legal norms repeats today. As the late nineteenth century started to experience an unraveling of the moral logic of the British Empire, it is hardly surprising that the alienated legal framework of Victorian possessions acquired a place in the fictions of dispossession produced by Britain's former imperial possessions.

"Third World" literatures of debt are very aware that the abstract worlds developed in imperial finance are disconnected from the social and cultural experiences they are said to reference. Moshin Hamid's 2013 novel *How to Get Filthy Rich in Rising Asia* is a mock-up of a financial self-help book with no advice and no address. The "you" the text speaks to is not the reader but rather a fictional "you" with a life story of his own, a dialogical doubling of the author: "We are nearing our end," the narrator warns, "you and I, and this self-help book too" (177). The story is not a "self-help" after all but rides a fictional plotline, where the "you" is given someone else's story, gaining leverage by borrowing against physical reality: "'If we don't borrow,' he says, 'we'll die'" (178). Teddy Wayne's 2010 novel *Kapitoil* relates the story of a coder from Qatar who, working in a New York bank and deciphering Jackson Pollock's philosophy, discovers an algorithm for investment returns that would also serve as an algorithm to end disease in the "Third World." His boss tries to entice him into signing over his intellectual property rights in order to bank on the algorithm's supercompetitive profit margins, but the coder refuses and returns to Qatar. Amitav Ghosh's 2008 novel *Sea of Poppies* recounts how the British Empire forced opium production on Asia by forcing debt onto their local rulers. "Your debts to my company," says the British merchant Mr. Burnham to the Raja, "would not be covered even by the sale of the estate" (119). In these novels, finance is what splits and alienates the subject, the point of irresolvable antagonism between the direction of profit and the space from where profit is drawn as debt, between the realities of the built world and the fictions of its promise.

"Third World" debt literature, though, does not begin post-2008. Wole Soyinka's 1965 play *The Road*, for example, tells of a group of Nigerian drivers, or touts, who steal the sign "BEND" by the side of the road and then resell the items left behind by those who crash and die as a result of the sign's removal. As with the legal protocols surrounding the property of Lizzie's diamonds, the sign is removed as a descriptor of the territory, and without that marking, the road itself becomes unpredictable, and life itself is indebted to the controllers of symbols. Whereas *The Road* is about the loss of metaphysical belonging with the postcolonial state corrupted by development, Kenyan Ngugi wa Thiong'o's 2006 novel *Wizard of the Crow* refashions *The Road*'s nationalist critique into a neoliberal mythology. *Wizard* is a comedy of errors telling of a fictional "Third World" nation trying to debt finance a large but useless project to build a replica of the biblical Tower of Babel in order to commemorate the corrupt Ruler and attract foreign investors. This novel mocks governance in the neoliberalized indebted nation by showing its state bureaucracies standing on fictions of power produced by the financial take-over of its sovereign institutions: the nation as such, like the sign "BEND" in *The Road*, is in a sense emptied of meaning and therefore agency as well. Straddling a time when finance was turning away from investments in production in order to focus on representations of value outside of production, these texts explore the nexus between increasing debt and the shrinking credibility of the promise of the material world, its cultures, and the lives of its producers.

J. P. Morgan's practice of putting the costs of accumulation onto a fictional character might apply not only to shell companies. Finance also depends on creating a character out of the "Third World" that would hold negative value as the "dump" of toxic value. The creation of the "indebted character" of the "Third World" is tied to a nineteenth-century construction of indebted persons as sitting in an off-kilter relation to the legal parameters of the citizen-persona most often marked by race or culture. My point in crossing from the Victorian novel into inflections of finance in a more contemporary novel and a play is to show how the "Third World" is constructed within narratives of debt as an unsignifiable object, a negative identity. Historian Peter James Hudson[4] has documented how Wall Street dominated the Caribbean, "guaranteed by force" (21), operating in a zone beyond legal reference that Hudson calls "racial capitalism," where "banking and finance capitalism also emerged as an *attack* on black bodies" (256). "Racial capitalism" developed first in the "loose regulatory environment" (25) of the American west, with high-risk investments fraudulently secured through land theft and dispossessions enabled by jurisdictional gaps and regulatory ambiguities. Banks acquired land by emptying it of its aboriginal inhabitants, using mortgages on the "financialized space" (24), operating between legality and illegality and guaranteeing the acquisitions through force. Just as financial abstractions such as mortgages were used to displace aboriginal holdings on land, the North American Trust Company, preceding the National City Bank, "leveraged the Cuban government deposits to finance personal enterprises" (39) and preempted Cuban sovereignty by rewriting Cuban constitutional law while supporting possibly illegal regimes.

"Third World" as an identity can be said to be retrofitted into the negativity of financial representations of value that debt introduces. Because the benefits of capital accumulation are removed and alienated from the place of their extraction, debt is what Lazzarato calls "asignifying semiotics," which "function whether or not they signify something for someone" (*Governing* 24). As Lazzarato goes on to explain, "In capitalism, sign flows (money, logarithms, diagrams, equations) act directly on material flows, bypassing signification, reference, and denotation, all of which are linguistic categories incapable of accounting for the operations of the capitalist machine" (*Governing* 24). That is to say that finance follows the logic of the "signifying economy" as analyzed by a whole host of structuralist and poststructuralist thinkers, such as Saussure, Lacan, Lévi-Strauss, Derrida, Barthes, Kristeva, Foucault, and Deleuze (Lazzarato's analysis builds mostly on the work of these final two). This critique taught generations of literary and cultural scholars that linguistic signs—words but also syntax, form, concept, and structure—were defined in relation to their difference from other linguistic signs rather than in relation to social relations in the world. Signs deferred engaging in objects indefinitely, postponing and then postponing again decisions on definitive, enduring meanings. The economic turn of this deferral of attributing absolute meaning or value is particularly evident in a neoliberal era, when institutions of state sovereignty, with their impetus toward development and their promise of progress, are being turned into financial products by financial actors and sold off to other financial bidders whose interests lie elsewhere. As in Cuba and Haiti, Hudson resumes, in Puerto Rico, "the City Bank served as the depository of government funds while hampering the development of a truly national institution" (265). Neoliberalism can be understood as a historical stage of capitalism that has turned away from workers, local cultures, and the commodity form, including social safety-net policies that support working lives, avoiding the slowdowns and stoppages entailed when capital needs workers to reproduce themselves for production. Neoliberalism thus forces debt on the "Third World" by its disinvestments in reproduction that make "Third World" countries into high-risk areas, increasing profitability.

David Harvey has dated this shift toward neoliberalism from the 1970s with the bankruptcy of New York City. Before then, deindustrialization, says Harvey, and the consequent depletion of the economic base (giving rise to the term *the urban crisis*) led to social unrest that was met with public spending to solve the problems. Richard Nixon, however, declared the end to the crisis in the early 1970s and diminished federal aid to the city. Though at first the banks were willing to cover the differences that ensued between spending and revenues, in 1975 Citibank decided to push the city into bankruptcy and then bailout, and other banks followed suit. The terms of the bailout were that the bankers "had first claim on city tax revenues in order to first pay off bondholders . . . The effect was to curb the aspirations of the city's powerful municipal unions, to implement wage freezes and cutbacks in public employment and social provision (education, public health, transport services), and to impose user fees (tuition was introduced into the CUNY [City University of New York] university system for the first time)" (Harvey 45). According to Harvey, "the Chicago boys" who followed Milton Friedman at the University of Chicago looked at this response to New York City's crisis in order to build the blueprint for their brand of neoliberalism. New York City's bankruptcy inspired the similar market fundamentalist reforms implemented in Chile under the regime of Augusto Pinochet, which would be the first iteration of Latin America's debt crisis in the 1980s. It also underlaid the market restructuring of New Orleans after Hurricane Katrina in 2005 and of Iraq after the US invasion of 2003. And, I would add, it closely resembles the transformations in sovereign control of institutions happening currently in the corporate-managerial take-over of Detroit's and Puerto Rico's governance. *Promissory Notes* explores the case of Puerto Rico to show how debt's construction of the "Third World" as a negative identity gives rise to material effects of neoliberal debt.

At the same time in the early 1970s, in the wake of successful decolonization struggles and national liberation movements in the 1960s, global economic relations were entering a new phase of capitalist organization. As economist Samir Amin argues, this new phase witnesses "the erosion of three subsystems that formed the basis of postwar [World War II] growth (the national welfare state in the West, the national bourgeois project of Bandung in the Third World, and Sovietism in the Eastern bloc)" (34). In all three of these geopolitical scenes, state power was considerably weakened, particularly in what is generally called its "soft arm," or its reproductive functions, in favor of its "strong arm," or military and security functions, including its functions in securing and strengthening the economic base of the political elites through the polarization of national income. This transfer of more of the national wealth toward the wealthy (through cuts to welfare and education, for example, and increases to military technologies, as well as tax policies and the like) resulted in a stagnation of wages across the spectrum and—at least in the West—an explosion of debt as workers made up for their loss of real income by borrowing.

The depletion of state reproductive power in the neoliberal West and in the US "urban crisis" thus paralleled the depletion of state power in the developmental state. As workers in the West borrowed against the losses of their share of the national wealth in the form of decreases to social spending, aid and assistance to social and government projects in formerly colonized states, states of the Global South, or (labor and raw material) supplier states also borrowed, often with strings attached to the loans that demanded even more austerity.[5] The emptying out of New York City's governing power by predatory financial profit seekers coincides with the same sorts of rearrangement of state redistribution in other places, and particularly in the "Third World," with the end of the development state and the rise of structural adjustment policies (SAPs) designed to manage debt, even at the expense of the population's economic well-being. Samir Amin enumerates the effects of structural adjustment as "a sharp increase in unemployment, a fall in the remuneration of work, an increase in food dependency, a grave deterioration of the environment, a deterioration in healthcare systems, a fall in admissions to educational institutions, a decline in the productive capacity of many nations, the sabotage of democratic systems, and the continued growth of external debt" (13). These are also structural adjustment's causes: the apparent expansion of the needs of the population fuels the claim of their exorbitant cost and the necessity of reining in the public spending on their behalf, even when the absence of capital investments or fair division of the profits produced the need for public spending in the first place. Neoliberalism's culture of debt appropriates increasingly more of the workers' share of the profits of their production: through debt, financial institutions are, more or less, *charging* workers for the right to collect their own wages.

*Promissory Notes* does not set out to blame literature for the financial crisis. It does, however, show literature's relevance to the political-economic situation that makes sense of debt. In a post-Saussurian, post-Lacanian understanding of the literary text, representation is put under the spotlight not as a worldly reflection but rather as, on the one hand, distanced from the world of social relations that is, on the other, pointing toward the creation of a world of social relations that could be. Marx explains that under capitalism, the product of production—which has in it a part of the life of the worker—is taken away from the producer, and this might be particularly true in neoliberal finance. Literature forces us to be wary of the way representation is removed from the context it affects, how it speaks and who controls that speaking, and how representation divides the sayable from the unsayable as well as the possible from the impossible. While politicians and pundits alike are telling us that the economy is a field that requires expertise to understand, that the only ones smart enough to fix the economic debacle are the same ones who were smart enough to have caused it, literature can play a pedagogical role through its deep, self-reflective analysis of representational abstraction and linguistic play as a technique of power. Literature teaches us, in fact, that representational forms, as sites of struggle (not just expertise), produce the worlds of social relations that they seem to reflect and that those with control over the representational instruments are the ones who get to decide what the future of social relations will be.

# CHAPTER 1

## FUTURES AND FICTIONS

### *The Right to Make Promises and the Object That Never Was*

Nietzsche teaches us that indebted men are not born but bred. Being bred "*with the right to make promises*" (57), indebted men are made to promise a "future in advance" (58) that is governed by the seeming "certainty" of calculation. Yet, for Nietzsche, debt introduces an epistemological uncertainty into the science of "certainty," because debt is antilife: it subordinates life to the "*exceptional conditions*" (76) of the law, and it punishes people for reasons that are "totally *indefinable*" and for outcomes that "elude definition" (80). Because of debt's relation to uncertainty, it is less a response to systems and more an excuse for power. In this view, debt is not an agent of need, a boost to development, or a reciprocal response to exchange (a system of equivalents) but rather a primary and unequalizing force that manufactures fear and guilt toward the ends of control, obedience, and subjection. As Maurizio Lazzarato interprets Nietzsche, "The importance of the debt economy lies in the fact that it appropriates and exploits both chronological labor time and *action*, non-chronological time, time as choice, decision" (*Indebted Man* 55), and, let us add, as theory (i.e., a reflection on the relationship between *what is* and *what appears*, between *what we know about what is* and *what we experience*, or between the "is" of describing the world and the "ought" of *what could be*).

In 2015, weeks before what was then a potential Puerto Rican massive loan default (the largest public loan default in history), Juan González delivered a speech at Columbia University (later replayed on *Democracy Now!*) in which he called PREPA—the Puerto Rican electric company[1]—"the Crown Jewels of Puerto Rico." What made González compare a public utility company to such reverenced, exclusive Victorian diamonds? In this chapter, I interpret Anthony Trollope's 1873 novel *The Eustace Diamonds* as giving a picture of financial representation as it applies to imperial culture at the historical moment just before the United States acquired Puerto Rico from Spain. I claim that Puerto Rico has a legal legacy in conversation with Victorian diamonds in that they both are objects around which circulates the irreconcilable question of debt. In other words, the Victorian diamond, like Puerto Rico, is a visible object—an asset—representing the possibility of a value that is *less than nothing* at a time when people were skeptical about trusting money as a representation of value referring to no material thing.[2] Fiction plays a historical role in creating belief in imaginary objects that do not exist, compelling a representational system divorced from correspondence to things and events while still producing value. Building on Mary Poovey's term *fictionalization*, whereby "the reader must be willing to extend to these [financial] abstractions a variant of the belief that she would extend to a fictional character" (*Genres* 142), I mean by *fictional capital* a genre of non-empirical but realistic representation, where the representational structure itself borrows from imaginative techniques, making the line between the actual legitimate or conventional imaginative projection and the deliberatively fake appearance of value blurry or altogether obsolete. Like fiction, money is just coming to be thought of as a thing representing something that, by definition, *is not*, never was, and might never be *there*.

Fictional capital today has become much more normalized, no longer needing pedagogical interventions most of the time. Or maybe people are learning to accept intermittent crises and the ensuing economic remedies—more deregulation, more austerity—that clear the ground for more upward redistributions of wealth, often under the guise of "job creation." As British novelist John Lanchester notes in his nonfiction book about the 2008 crisis, *I.O.U.*, "When I first began to study the world of the City, I found it hard to come to grips with the idea that financial instruments are 'invented,' cooked up in the same ways as works of art" (57).[3] This is true not only of financial power but also of legislative and juridical power as it determines how value can be extracted from assets. A US example is the landmark 2010 case *Citizens United vs. FEC* (Federal Election Committee), when the US Supreme Court decided to reconfirm the idea that corporations were like legal people, subject to the same civil rights and property protections as ordinary citizens, including freedom of speech and, by extension, freedom of religious belief. In the same gesture, the Supreme Court defined money as speech and spending money as exercising a First Amendment right. In other words, corporations have been legally established, as they first were in the late nineteenth century, as characters, often with imagined composite personalities and participating in narratives of aggrievement, language acquisition, and subject construction.

This is not the only place where the economy functions through characterization and narrativization. As Lanchester explains, the credit default swaps (CDS), or "synthetic collateralized debt obligations," which played such a heavy role in the 2008 financial crisis, also operated by creating a false company identity. In these trades, the bank issuing the loan would set up an offshore shell company, or special purpose vehicle (SPV), that would assume the risk, insuring the loan so that the bank would be able to remove the loan from its balance sheets, increasing the bank's leverage and reducing its tax burden. Banks that, by the Basel rules, were obligated to maintain a certain percentage of reserves against total loan amounts, could extend more credit. "You could use your capital very effectively over and over again," concludes Lanchester, "because you needed to post only part of the capital as collateral against the risk of default" (73). By creating these fictional personas, the bank was able to issue loans at no risk while diminishing its public responsibilities. In addition, underlying credit swaps was a system of insurance whose prices were set according to inadequate correlative data (or measurements of how their prices rose and fell in relation to others in securities markets) rather than on the historical data—whether or not, for example, the bundled mortgages were likely to be paid back. This meant that the uncertainties of what the future might bring were filled in by bell curve calculations and, as Lanchester continues, "mathematical models [that] simply didn't work in a crisis" (162). Such securitization was premised, therefore, on making loans to people not by determining the quality of their character, credibility, past behavior, and likelihood of payback but rather by insinuating composite probabilities as character construction, where risk assessments could be divided up into particular product lines and combined into financial risk patterns or personalities and then ranked accordingly.

The history of Puerto Rico's financial colonization follows a course where aspects of cultural character are projected onto the island and measured against stock characters of probable creditworthiness. Evolving as a political and legislative entity inside the history of financial authority's ascendance, Puerto Rico assumes a fictional character as investment risk. Puerto Rico's case is certainly one where a character was produced that would augment the level of risk to make it a "good investment" and a site of excessive profits.

The contemporary situation of debt in Puerto Rico reveals that debt is a product of legalistic maneuvering rather than a result of irresponsible spending. Puerto Rican debt was blown out of proportion after the expiration of a 2006 tax abatement policy when 936 firms left the island, and investors convinced the government to issue municipal bonds—some with the highest yields—to make up the difference, often bypassing legal limits. PREPA, González continues, is able to issue billions of dollars in private bonds to investors living outside of Puerto Rico. Under the provisions of Puerto Rico's 1952 Constitution, available resources would go to servicing debt obligations first, making every single person on the island responsible for paying the debt through austerity cuts. PREPA-issued bonds are backed as well by other public entities like the Government Development Bank and the Highways and Transportation Authority, creating a situation in which "everything in Puerto Rico is bonded and is owed to someone—to someone outside the country," says González. A default could mean a loss in funding for roads and schools, as that public money would be transferred to the private investors as a priority in times of crisis. The economic setup—where Puerto Rico is kept permanently in debt because the more it collects, the more it owes to private investors living elsewhere—means Puerto Rico is permanently and essentially made unequal as a matter of its existence, as the debt structuring prohibits its sovereign control over its own financial governance. The United States controls Puerto Rico's borders and tariffs because it is part of the United States but only confers partial citizenship and property rights because it is not a state. How did this situation come about?

Puerto Rico has a special status that is both inside and outside US law. This is González's point. Its colonial legacy gives it that special status, where its fit with US civil rights, commercial, and sovereign protections has always been highly contested. Puerto Rico, says González, is in a "unique situation" because it is subjected to unique and unprecedented legislation: unlike US states, it has no congressional representation; unlike US municipalities, it has—since legislation passed in 1984—no Chapter 9 bankruptcy provisions, while it offers insured and "triple tax-exempt bonds," which means exemption from paying local, state, and federal taxes on income from bonds, an instrument, unavailable anywhere else in the United States, that helps divest the Puerto Rican treasury. As Mary Williams Walsh in the *New York Times* explains, no one "can tax the interest that Puerto Rico pays its investors" because of a law from 1917 that was meant to push internal development in order to show Puerto Rico as outshining Soviet-backed Cuba. Puerto Rico is exceptional: "If it is neither a state nor an independent nation," González queries, "what exactly is Puerto Rico?"

González argues that Puerto Rico achieves this special status through its colonial history, and to back this argument, he cites US Court of Appeals judge Juan Torruella, the only Hispanic judge ever to serve on the First Circuit. Torruella notes that the debate over Puerto Rican annexation after the Spanish-American War made the application of US law irregular, where Puerto Rico's relation to the name "America" was set in disarray on the basis of racial difference. Where one side argued that US law applied to all those on US territory and that there was therefore a constitutional obligation to make territories into states, the other side—citing the famous 1857 *Dred Scott* case, in which it was decided that former slaves could not be US citizens or stand in court—declared the permanent inequality of the island's inhabitants due to their inability to assimilate the values and conduct assumed to be shared by all US citizens as their identity. "The inhabitants are of wholly different races of people from ours," Thomas Spight, representative of Mississippi, reasoned. "They have nothing in common with us and centuries can not assimilate them . . . They can never be clothed with the rights of American citizenship" (as cited in Torruella 35). The customs of the inhabitants of Puerto Rico, thought a contributing professor in the *Harvard Law Review* comparing the case to Florida, were not translatable into the language of the Bill of Rights: "Those ten amendments as a whole are so peculiarly and so exclusively English that an immediate and compulsory application of them to ancient and thickly settled Spanish colonies would furnish striking proof of our unfitness to govern dependencies, or to deal with alien races" (as cited in Torruella 27). As the debate shows, the law maneuvers maladroitly to create a representation of difference within but outside the universalizing abstraction of citizenship. The debate also suggests that categories for knowing and experiencing social existence—like "America"—do not necessarily have obvious social referents or a secure framing of belonging.

According to González, this special in-between status—being both inside and outside the law's abstractions—weakens Puerto Rico's sovereign claim over its borders and productive enterprises and allows the rules of capital accumulation to be set by those outside the island who serve to profit but who have no reason to be responsive or sympathetic to local needs. For example, shipping in and out of Puerto Rico, unlike any of the neighboring islands, is restricted by the 1920 Jones Act (protecting the US merchant marine within US waters) to US-constructed ships, costing Puerto Rico, says González, $567 million extra a year, even though the companies are using Greek and Cypriot crews that have low labor costs. "Only those parts of the Constitution apply in U.S. territorial possessions that Congress chooses to apply," González summarizes. "Puerto Rico . . . belonged to but was not part of the United States." Puerto Rico is set up as unequal by its uncertain, fictional relation to a legal system meant to assume that all are equals before its law. As Nelson Denis writes in *The Nation*, "This is where our Commonwealth relationship to the United States has gotten us: an island of beggars and billionaires, owned by absentee landlords, fought over by lawyers, clerked by politicians." Puerto Rico is being punished for the inequality imposed on it from the start.

Debt in Puerto Rico, as González describes its history, is created by an uncertain relation to the law or to the status of the law and its application, and it actually produces uncertainty as part of the legal structure to accommodate a necessary inequality. If the law is meant to apply to all equally, then raising the question of to whom it applies presumes an embedded inequality. If the word *citizen* is meant to refer to an actual body-in-the-world, then questioning its referential application also serves to question that body's existence for that world. Because of the question of whether law applies, the law can apply selectively to an imagined general or ideal designation, or the law can be decided singularly, for this case only. That is, debt is attributed to objects whose uncertain legal categorization makes them possibly subject to authoritative controls, decision making, and opportunistic gaming rather than bureaucratic regulation or universalist abstract principles, as liberalism would warrant or as the category of "citizen" implies. I am not insinuating that debt has no material effects—on the contrary! Puerto Rico—like the category "students," for example—is identified and maintained as indebted, permanently, in the very way it enters into social, symbolic, and political relations. Debt is part of Puerto Rico's historical identity, its (post)coloniality.

González's use of Victorian diamonds as a metaphor for this situation of debt is revealing. In this chapter, I argue that Trollope's diamonds appeared as an incoherence in the legal coding at the time—between heirloom and commodity, between material object and financial product—in ways similar to the Puerto Rico that González describes. In such situations, authorities take control of time via representation: that is, they take control of the uncertainties by securitizing them in stable representations of future profits in the present.

Though much scholarship traces the political and cultural history of Latin America from Spanish conquest, interpreting conquest as the rupture out of which modern identities and class relations were forged, Torruella and González read the history of the Spanish Caribbean—particularly Cuba and Puerto Rico—and the Philippines as it starts to be inscribed in US constitutional law after the Spanish-American War in 1898, in the time of financialization. In this historical lineage, the rupture was not a one-time event that transformed what came after but rather is ongoing and continually reinstituted, even in everyday practices, whenever US laws move to reinscribe these colonies/protectorates for policies of deeper economic accumulations. As mandated by the Treaty of

Paris, the legal, civil, and political status of Puerto Rican territory "shall be determined by Congress" (qtd. in Torruella 24). In a debate that ensued the year after the Treaty of Paris in the *Harvard Law Review*, experts pointed out that unlike in European conquests, US expansion should be guided by the Constitution. The "temporary" denial of citizenship rights to territories was therefore considered "abnormal" (25); moving expediently toward statehood was therefore necessary. Today, statehood is still on hold.

The US institutionalization of Puerto Rico, as it starts at the turn of the twentieth century, might therefore be recognized in parallel to a moment when British Victorians were starting to take account, at the end of the nineteenth century, of a burgeoning financialization that had not yet acquired a matching legal structure. Anthony Trollope's 1873 *The Eustace Diamonds* was a pedagogical or informational novel that sought to teach its readers how to negotiate a financial system that was yet unfamiliar and increasingly confusing in the mid- to late nineteenth century. The reason to write on *The Eustace Diamonds* now is that it is all about money, and it is about money at a particular time when money was coming to be understood as a means to finance[4] but also as something that needed to be explained. Representative of a transition in what was understood as a legal form of property, Trollope's diamonds fall both inside and outside the contemporaneous terms by which property could be recognized, known, determined, regulated, valued, and therefore owned and exchanged, like Puerto Rico today (also like credit default swaps and mortgage-backed securities today). Also like Puerto Rico, the inequality of the diamonds to legal property descriptors and categories invites legalistic maneuvering to control, through authority, the terms of ownership and future possession. Without determination as a type of property recognizable within property law, the diamonds—or Puerto Rico—can be treated as a legal exception, a negative value, an inequality, an uncertainty, a risk, or debt.

Caught in a transitional moment when property as land is beginning to be overshadowed by financial capital—mobile instruments of value capture dependent on conventions of representation: balance sheets, bank accounts, coins, paper, stocks, letters of exchange, bills, contracts, checks, and so on—*The Eustace Diamonds* traces a concept of the economy dependent on information, where types can be recognized because they can be equated with other types, as abstractions. Yet the abstracted informational codes are often inadequate for identifying the particular objects to be owned and valued. *The Eustace Diamonds* makes debt into an object, but an indeterminate one, specific but undefinable and unnamable. Like Puerto Rico and its relation to the category of "citizen," the diamonds as debt cannot be equalized with symbolic representations of existing types of possessions; proving the law as un-universalizable, they mark the ones who hold them as untrustworthy and not wholly what they seem to be. Debt reveals the limitations of property in the language that determines it as property—that is, in the language of money. Like González's questions about Puerto Rico, *The Eustace Diamonds*, then, asks, If they can't be owned or traded, if they are neither land nor movable commodities, if they are neither heirlooms nor gifts nor gold nor paraphernalia, if they cannot be said definitively to belong to anyone in particular, if they therefore have a negative value for those in possession of them, then what exactly are the Eustace diamonds?

Authoritarian imposition was exactly what became transparent in Puerto Rico when an unelected emergency manager control board—referred to as "La Junta"—was appointed by Congress under Title III, with a law titled PROMESA[5] meant to reassure hedge funds, vulture funds, and other investors who thought Chapter 9 was unfavorable to them. Drafted by Republican Speaker of the House Paul Ryan, Title III—or PROMESA—only applies to Puerto Rico as an exception. What Ed Morales of *The Nation* has called a "throwback to the early days of US colonial rule, when the governor was a US military officer appointed by the president," PROMESA passed with bipartisan support under the Obama administration and with continued support under Trump and gives Puerto Rico's elected governor no control over the restructuring, the largest in history—nine times larger than Detroit's. Except for one resident member, the board would be staffed principally by non–Puerto Rican businesspeople living off the island—six of the seven chosen by Congress—to redistribute Puerto Rico's assets so that the debts could be paid, taking money from teacher and state worker pensions, Medicare, university budgets, schools, health care, housing, and the like (e.g., the minimum wage would be reduced to $4.25/hour). As David Graeber reflects, "Debt peonage continues to be the main principle of recruiting labor globally: either in the literal sense, in much of East Asia or Latin America, or in the subjective sense, whereby most of those working for wages or even salaries feel that they are doing so primarily to pay off interest-bearing loans" (368–69). This is particularly true, he continues, for countries and regions under the control of International Monetary Fund (IMF) austerity policies. Debt interrupts the uncertainty opened in the present by the future—the potential for public roads and schools, the lives extended by health care—by subjecting it to the demands of the present, as the command of payback takes back authority over the uncertain, the undefinable, the risky, and the theoretical.

## DIAMONDS

*The Eustace Diamonds* treats as narrative a transition in the concept of property the necklace foregrounds: types of property that depend on a distance or noncomplicity between the object and its representation (as with credit, currency, and debt). These instruments are based on fictions of value—belief systems and trust—rather than on inheritance[6] or referentiality.[7] "If a thing is a man's own," contemplates the main character, Lizzie Eustace, "he can give it away;—not a house, or a farm, or a wood, or anything like that; but a thing he can carry with him—of course he can give it away" (Trollope, *Eustace* 94). Well, it is not that simple, as Lizzie learns in the course of the novel. *The Eustace Diamonds* is Lady Lizzie Eustace's story, with Lizzie's character modeled on Becky Sharp of Thackeray's 1848 satiric novel *Vanity Fair* (though Trollope's hatred of satire is well known). When her father the admiral dies and leaves her in debt, caused in part by her obsession with wearing fake jewelry, Lizzie resolves her financial burdens by marrying Sir Florian Eustace, who dies a year later, bequeathing a lifetime income to her and his heir. Part of Eustace's possessions had been a diamond necklace that he may have given to Lizzie as a gift but did not mention in his will, yet she claims it as hers. The Eustace estate lawyers try to take it back into the family estate. For this, they need to determine if it could be said to be a family heirloom, a chattel, a gift, or a piece of paraphernalia; whether she could legally sell the diamonds off; and whether her son's rights to property limit her own. The novel obsesses over the status of the diamonds—a status that remains categorically indeterminable and is never resolved.

The question the diamonds pose is if, without referring to an object in a line of exchange, money can lie. Lizzie is the character in which this question is most prevalent because her class background jars heavily against her class aspirations, so she is always in the process of appearing to be of greater value than she is by her lying. As readers, we are supposed to hate everything about Lizzie: her tenacity about having the diamonds as much as her taste for what Trollope sees as the false floweriness of lyric poetry like in Byron, Shelley, and Tennyson: she, like the capital she represents, is shallow, crafty, clever, and deceptive. Her claim to her fortune is, for the most part, a pretense against which she overspends, and displaying the diamonds, she overstates her wealth to lure a series of indebted men into making marriage offers, just as Romantic poetry overstates its value. "She would tell any number of lies to carry a point," Trollope begins his description. "It was said of her that she cheated at cards. In backbiting no venomous old woman between Bond Street and Park Lane could beat her" (*Eustace* 42), and Trollope's venom continues relentlessly. Lizzie's financial failings contribute to Trollope's depictions of her moral failings.[8] Though, as Alan Roth writes in the *Stanford Law Review*, "professors will never concoct a fact pattern so compelling" (879) as *The Eustace Diamonds*, much of what obscures the factual attribution of the diamonds as property is Lizzie's lying: for example, the diamonds are more likely to be "chattels" if given to her in Scotland with the rest of the properties in the Eustace Scottish castle, so she says that they were, and the writing in the jeweler's ledger is smudged so the potential lie cannot be proven right or wrong. As Walter Kendrick expresses it, Lizzie "is Trollope's attempt to represent realistically the opposite of realism, to appropriate and condemn a way of using language which is inimical to that of the Trollopian novel" (137). She even steals her own diamonds the first time and then lies to the police (and everybody else); when the diamonds disappear the second time, she again lies to the police. Lizzie's falsifications about the diamonds—their whereabouts, whether they have been promised, whether she has them—make the diamonds into pure representation, with their reference point and terms of possession in constant movement. Contingently, her fictional claims threaten to expose as false (or moveable) the authority, morals, and social understanding to which she—as well as the social class to which she aspires—pretends. As an imposter, she implies they all are imposters and that the objects that confer their status are, possibly like the diamonds, just paste.

Like financial capital as well, Lizzie—who is an orphan and then a widow—gets passed from hand to hand without anyone being able to hold onto her. Interpreting her as free of immediate kinship and so with more than normal social agency than allotted to other women, Kathy Psomiades summarizes, "Lizzie is bad not only because she openly places her charms on the marriage market, but because she doesn't have the value she claims to have. Her value is exchange value" (95). She is the prototype of what Marx describes as debt: carried by "dissimulation, hypocrisy and sanctimoniousness," she makes herself into "counterfeit coin" to "obtain credit by stealth, by lying" ("Comments on James Mill") or by fiction. Lizzie's character is contrasted with her nemesis and childhood friend, Lucy Morris—referred to at multiple points as "good as gold" (e.g., Trollope, *Eustace* 305, 309, 314) or a "firm rock" (151)—who, likewise orphaned, is ugly and poor though virtuous and trustworthy and whose sincere and worthy engagement to Frank Greystock, a Conservative member of Parliament, Lizzie nearly ruins. In contrast to Lizzie, Lucy seems true because her value does refer to an object, and one that is most solid: "There was a reality and a truth about her [Lucy]," Frank meditates, "which came home to him and made themselves known to him as firm rocks which could not be shaken" (151). As Lizzie ruminates, she "knew that she was paste and knew that Lucy was real stone" (628). Unlike Lizzie, we *can* trust what Lucy says and sympathize with it. "If Lucy Morris ruled the world," Kendrick concludes, "there would be no novels in it" (156). A lawyer, Greystock himself had risen to political prominence by "saving" the gold standard against encroachments that the City of London was trying to inflict through legal action; he defends the Bank of England by reconstructing its bullion cellars (67). Much of the novel takes place in the suspension of Frank's promise to Lucy Morris, a promise that—like debt or credit—inserts a delay or anticipation about whether his word is real and he will return to her, as, the novel keeps reminding us, he clearly should (and eventually does a good seven hundred pages later). Trollope directly labels Frank's promise to Lucy as a debt: "Whatever might be his future lot in life, he owed it to her to share it with her, and if he evaded his debt, he would be a traitor and a miscreant" (573). Yet unlike Lizzie's debt, Frank returns to Lucy after a time; though not heroic, he eventually proves himself true. Whereas Frank fulfills this promise by returning to a future with Lucy, Trollope leaves Lizzie in a debt whose future promise is unforeseeable.

The issue for Trollope is the troublesome relationship between fiction and finance. Fiction can be two things. It can be deliberate, where reality is intentionally distorted through false representation and fraud, or it can be nondeliberate, where the representation is excessive to its intention because the reality that the representation is meant to capture does not rest easily or exhaust itself within the representation's referential structure. Mary Poovey is concerned with attempts leading up to the age of finance to distinguish between the modern fact—true to nature, focused on particulars—and what she sometimes calls "figurative language" or rhetoric and other times calls theory, generalized abstractions, systems, or models (*Modern Fact* 6). Finance also demanded an accounting of types of financial fiction that shared figuration but had different intentions and effects: credit, fraud, and risk, for example. The potential that value could be imaginary—not held in things but projected through representations—means that future value cannot totally be captured and controlled in the present. Financiers, of course, want to minimize potential loss or risk by setting up secure fictional representations of debt in a way that limits their own responsibility and extends the debtor subject and the creditor-debtor relationship, as represented in the present, into the future as far as possible. As Trollope shows in the character of Lizzie Eustace, however, Victorians were not totally convinced of securing all future possibility.

In finance, representations of value refer to other representations. If, as Poovey contests, the credit economy of the nineteenth century "did not explicitly or consistently differentiate between objective data, which seemed simply to reflect the natural world, and imaginative or rhetorical representations, which clearly elaborated or transformed the observable world" (*Genres* 90), then how can the necessary fictions of financial capital—the tools for representing value as data or things—be distinguished from pure fraud and deceit? Through Lizzie, Trollope marks a confusion between representations that are deliberatively deceitful and appropriative, such as fraud, and those that are sympathetic and truthful and therefore good for the right kind of finance. She is then punished in order to set her apart as bad fiction, as debt, and to clarify that these untruthful fictions are different from fictions of real value even as they appear, formally, the same.[9] My contention here is that Lizzie, like the diamonds, shares the theoretical character of money as debt; she *is* debt: she introduces and emphasizes the idea that money is not what it seems (it might not be *anything*), that (unlike Frank) it cannot fulfill its promise by returning to partnership with the object, that it could be exposed as mere representation—as fiction—and that its representation can only be made a credible and real value through an authoritative imposition, often violent.

In *The Eustace Diamonds*, Trollope creates a plot around the problem of property in relation to a rising awareness that value is tied to imaginative representations—or figuration—rather than things. Though some of the characters seek to ground the necklace's value in the rock-hard solidity of the family name to which it belongs, the necklace cannot sustain a connection to that name.[10] The necklace moves among national locations, definitions, legal interpretations, settings, pawnshops, politics, allegations of forgery, and holders' intents, acquiring different types of meaning in different contexts and in relation to different symbols. "Would the Law do a service, do you think," asks the legal expert Dove, rhetorically, "if it lent its authority to the special preservation in special hands of trinkets only to be used in vanity and ornament? Is that a kind of property over which an owner should have a power of disposition more lasting, more autocratic, than is given him even in regard to land? The land, at any rate, can be traced. It is a thing fixed and known. A string of pearls is not only alterable, but constantly altered, and cannot easily be traced" (Trollope, *Eustace* 295). Yet the lawyers never fully ascertain that the diamonds *are not* that kind of property. Like land, the diamonds seem to be weighty, as when the tall footman lifts the iron box made to keep the necklace, he buckles "as though it were a thing so heavy that he could hardly stagger along with it" (435). Fastening the necklace around her companion Miss Macnulty's neck, Lizzie says, "How do you feel, Julia, with an estate upon your neck? Five hundred acres at twenty pounds an acre" (323). Lizzie, on the other hand, hangs "them loose in her hand" and tosses them around like "any indifferent feminine bauble" (322). We soon learn, when the box is stolen and forced open, that—heavy or light—the box is empty.[11] While traveling, Lizzie carries the box holding the diamonds sometimes on her lap, sometimes under her feet, where it is an obstruction to her comfort, or hypervisible and drawing attention, although the box is meant to make the diamonds invisible and unattainable. Then the diamonds disappear, and the plotline seems unsure about how to proceed, eventually proceeding as though they are still there and then as though they are not there. Are the diamonds an object of value or are they an empty representation? As a hardened representation of an absence or transparent lack of substance—the main character's debt—the necklace suggests a persistent impossibility of identity between value and its representation as well as between Lizzie and the class to which she seeks to belong.

Critics have noted this problem of "class imposter" also being a theme in Trollope's 1876 novel *The Prime Minister*. A foreigner with no known parentage or country of origin, Ferdinand Lopez tries to break his way into English elite society by speculating on risky financial enterprises that fail. Lopez even succeeds in marrying one of the daughters of these elite classes. "A trope for the market" (79), as Audrey Jaffe calls him, Lopez's "admission to polite society threatens its solid values: not because that society doesn't 'know' . . . what kind of a man he is, but rather because it cannot locate the line he has crossed, nor can it draw one that will keep him out" (78). The difference with *The Eustace Diamonds*, which comes out three years earlier, is that finance does not appear as shady transactions on the exchange but rather as an object—an object that is simultaneously visible and invisible, an object that appears solid when it is not, an object whose value oscillates and whose ownership is multiple,[12] an object made untrustworthy because of its association with a woman with no relatives whose social position is never quite clear. The diamonds seem to be a device that calls out for a literary narrative to develop in order to stabilize its many meanings within a context where many contradicting interests are staking a claim.

The necklace adopts so many guises that characters question if its substance is original, bought and passed down by the grandfather Eustace; a fake, "no more than paste" (Trollope, *Eustace* 495); or replaced since the original acquisition. The question of how to establish value without referring to a specific, clear substance is thus the quest and the central question of the novel. The desire that language—in this case, the name—should be golden or solid as land (i.e., that it should secure the status of the object, its value and credibility in the object) is not confined to the constant scolding of Lizzie for not being true or for being too engaged in poetic literature. The novel's technique is to merge its fictional narration into other forms of writing, forms of writing that refer to actual objects in the world, an extranovelistic social world of correspondences, pamphlets, court cases, legal decisions, everyday communications, and informational exchanges: letters, reports, legal opinions, and so on. Information is diegetic, a plot device that explicates the economy of the intrigue and bleeds into the fictional narration to make it seem the style of a narrator with expert knowledge of the objects of his study. The disembodied narrative voice is able to blend into a bureaucratic voice and then extricate itself into a type of fiction that looks at the actions from outside, explaining and commenting.

The informational prose is differentiated from the romance or the flourishes of lyric poetry that Lizzie attributes to the literary/poetic but also integrated into the prose structure of Trollope's narrative, both being voices that explain. The factual, commercial, or informational often is invoked through mentioning names, years, prices, geographical places, legal precedents, or numbers referring to weighty objects: for example, "In 1674, Lord Keeper Finch declared that he would never allow paraphernalia, except to the widow of a nobleman. But in 1721 Lord Macclesfield gave Mistress Tipping paraphernalia to the value of £200" (*Eustace* 263). This turn toward the informational reveals two assumptions: (1) that Trollope is aware that the turns and twists of a novel about finance are not automatically understood by his readers so that they need signposts and pedagogical guidance that contextualize and explicate the plot to make readers see the diamonds as value of a certain complicated sort and (2) that Trollope understands the direct referential quality of information to be not the only producer of value in finance.

Informational realism, or direct reference, is insufficient to its task of representing value in objects in the logic of *The Eustace Diamonds*. Even so, Lucy wants to trust it: "There wasn't a word in it [Greystock's speech in Parliament, in favor of the Indian Sawab] that didn't seem to me to be just what it ought to be" (Trollope, *Eustace* 103). Lucy, however, does not convince even herself: "Was there any difference between a lie and an untruth?" she asks (299) in response to Lord Fawn's criticism of the speech (more on the Sawab below). The word *lie*, she thinks, implies an intention or an interest, yet could she consider that there was something intentionally deceptive in what Lord Fawn had just said? If she used the word the way "the world" (299) used it, could she trust the word? Suggested in Lucy's own thoughts is a conviction that language itself could be deceptive or fictional—especially when considering that it exists in a world of social transactions—and that the intention of the language would therefore not necessarily be the same as the speaker's intention. Ironically, Greystock's speech is a historical text that—unlike letters and lawyers' opinions and requests for money—is not reproduced as part of the narrative, so a major moment referred to in the text's evaluation of the truth in representation is missing, like the diamonds.

The narrative voice repeats Lucy's gesture of questioning the relationship among an object, its value, the truth of its representation, and the credibility of the informational language in which that representation is embedded. "We will tell you the story of Lizzie Greystock [Lizzie's family name—she is Frank's cousin] from the beginning," begins the novel in the narrator's voice, "but we will not dwell over it at great length, as we might do if we loved her" (39). Then, for some seven hundred pages, the narrator dwells over Lizzie as though "we" loved her. Here, the problem is pushed out to systemic levels, modeling its realism on the economic logic of sympathy that "portrays the real as both fictive and sympathetic" (Greiner 10), making the community of "we" from an imaginative projection. According to Rae Greiner, in the nineteenth century, literature evolved from the cognitive model of Adam Smith's moral philosophy of sympathy, involving an "exchange of imagined feeling" (4) that depended on a distance from identification. "These writings form a tradition," writes Greiner, "that portrays sympathy as a mental action involving the creation and exchange of imagined feeling, a way of sharing attitudes and modes of thought independent of the need to verify another's feeling" (4). The narrative voice of sympathy works because other people's feelings can be equal to his own, but as a form of representation, the narrative voice of sympathy is unequal to its representations, blocked from total identification. Trollope's narrative voice in *The Eustace Diamonds* shares the form of property law, as Dove describes it, trying to find similarities between the abstractions and categories for property and the property to be known and valued.

For Adam Smith, sympathy, as Greiner explains it, can only be felt when it is apart from the body, ideational before it affects physical feeling, so it requires distance. Something that touches your body does not induce sympathetic feeling; rather, an action you see whose expressive context you can imagine and share is the pretext for sympathy. Trollope asks his readers to sympathize with his plot by staging his characters in moral contemplation, mentally weighing choices and potential outcomes, responses, and moral judgments of their actions; the readers are encouraged not to attribute "good" or "evil" to a specific character but rather to reflect with the various characters on the possible implications of where their actions might narratively lead. Sympathy asks people to share in a fellow feeling with others but restricts access and identification to such feeling because you can never know: you can "go along with" their sentiments, passions, and sufferings without completely knowing the emotions, a type of "mental companionship" (Greiner 16) open to imaginative social interactions, affective connections, and virtual projections that cannot be reduced to a physical form. Sympathy models a social field of interaction with anonymous, distant others with whom we can find in common an affective, nonempirical relation with things.

Trollope's narrator in *The Eustace Diamonds* personifies this tradition. The narrator is not a character yet often behaves like one; has no body but seems present in scenes; has a consciousness apart from the characters' but is able to enter into and recreate the characters' thoughts even as he is able to stand outside, judge, and evaluate these thoughts; moves from one character's thoughts to another; is—in short—a multiplicity of subjects gathered into a mobile and seemingly singular though fictional social persona without a body. He is a virtual voice—impersonal, disembodied, changeable, judging, interpenetrating. The "we" that the narrative voice sometimes invokes as the storyteller appears as a sum of social positions, overlapping interests, and shared feelings. Sympathy here appears as a smooth sharing of subjective representations, where one subject position easily reflects another. In the chapter called "Too Bad for Sympathy," the narrator gives the reader instructions on how to read sympathetically. Do not think, he instructs, that literature identifies moral or immoral intentions and teaches moral behavior as does the Romantic and lyrical poetry that Lizzie reads. Romance, he goes on, presents heroes and villains whom we can care for because of their clearly readable intentions—for example, says the narrator, a "man carried away by abnormal appetites" who "may of course commit murder, or forge bills, or become a fraudulent director of a bankrupt company" (Trollope, *Eustace* 354). The distinction Trollope makes is between bills, for example, that are, like lyric, intentionally falsified (what Lucy might call "lies") and the value that gathers onto an object through its sympathies, its multiplying interests. The novel of sympathy thus appears, says Trollope's narrator, like the training ground for the financial marketplace.

Lizzie, on the other hand, is a negativity within the sympathetic narrative—the narrator cannot decide on her intention, cannot find "fellow feeling." Whereas when Lucy cries, thinks Frank, "a tear would sparkle, the smallest drop, a bright liquid diamond that never fell" (212), with Lizzie, the tears came too and "he partly believed the falsehood" (212). "The guiding motive of her conduct," he concludes, "was the desire to make things seem to be other than they were. To be always acting a part rather than living her own life was to be everything" (212). Unlike Lucy with her diamond tears that create an expressive context through which trust and feeling can be shared, Lizzie is inscrutable. The difference between Lizzie's inscrutability and the sympathy of "we" is, though, sometimes itself inscrutable, like the difference between Romantic poetry and the novel with its information. Like the lyric, debt as diamonds *looks like* a valuable substance but *acts like* a negative process, chipping away at the certainty, transparency, and intentionality of the community "we" that Lizzie may be part of as well as the name "Eustace," just as Lizzie forges feeling intentionally and so may contribute to but often disrupts sympathetic exchange.

Linked to literature, the fakeness or fictional quality of money as representation has two contradictory repercussions. First, Romantic-lyrical or popular literature, lying, debt, and femininity might appear as deceits that threaten morality and sympathy, the seeming permanence of social hierarchies, and faith in the stability of meaning in things. Such intentional artistry allows those who did not inherit names and power to act as though they did, mimicking the conduct of the landholding and political classes (or even their tears) and so making uncertain and discontinuous what was known to be the concrete reality of power. Or, second, representation itself was unintentionally excessive to the object because the object invited multiple sympathies or imaginative projections of other people's emotions that resisted identification. While Trollope defends the opposition between realism and romance, finance shared the effects but not the intentions of forgery (attributed to romance). In other words, finance stood in as the moral alibi for forgery: it could be confused with forgery because it combined a sympathetic mixture of intentions, some good and some bad. As I show below, colonization shores up such financial value.

## DISCIPLINE

For Mary Poovey, in the late eighteenth and early nineteenth centuries, an expertise in understanding and developing modes for analyzing imaginative writing is separated from an expertise in quantitative study of the economy—a "fact/fiction continuum" (*Genres* 77) (or divide), where what could be counted as "fact" "borrowed features from imaginative writing in order to give readers what no numbers could provide" (*Genres* 274).[13] By alluding to representation as a problem, Trollope—as one of Poovey's examples—presents aesthetic and moral narrative sympathies as literary checks on the unvirtuous dangers and corruptions that money unleashes as it represents value that is not yet there. Such novels, says Poovey, "look at *how* information is conveyed, *who* conveys it, and *where* it surfaces instead of taking it at face value, instead of treating it *as* information" (*Genres* 366). In *The Eustace Diamonds*, information connects to the object in a similar way that Kant relates reflective judgment to the beautiful object. Lizzie's diamonds are neither heirloom nor paraphernalia nor movable commodity but may be any of these, and we will never know, so that the object floats around looking for its definitional concept, which does not exist and needs to be created. Empire in *The*

*Eustace Diamonds* has a similar pathway through Kant's reflective judgment, where the (beautiful) object does not fit prior categories of cognitive representation and understanding and so demands a recirculation of the authority of those categories.[14]

Modernist critics have faulted Victorian literature, and realist novels in particular, for provincialism: an inability of the realist form to account for the global turn. Joe Cleary, for example, writes that "England and France in the nineteenth century produced between them scarcely a handful of major novels that directly engaged the business of empire" (259).[15] Following Fredric Jameson, who sees modernism and postmodernism alike, in contrast to realism, as an expansion of culture over "the yet untheorized original space of some new 'world system' of multinational or late capitalism" (*Postmodernism* 50), such accounts distinguish modernism for developing techniques that could account for imperialist financial expansion, privileging modernism as posing an aesthetic demand for Europe's coming to awareness of its empire's moral predicaments. As Lauren Goodlad responds, however, such readings, underscored by such influential scholars as Jameson, set "the stage for an interpretation of Modernism as offering a necessary break" (29) in both artistic and political understanding, patting the twentieth century—and modernism—on the back for its more global ethics. Such literary histories, says Goodlad, bury the "geopolitical aesthetic" of the nineteenth century under the rubric of progress.

In contrast to such modernist triumphalism, Victorian literary historians want to push backward the modernist transition to moments when the nineteenth century became aware of the weakening of the traditional markers of authority, opening the doors to linguistic and structural experimentation and signifying play. Connecting literary developments to such historical moments as the bursting of financial bubbles (e.g., in 1825, 1857, and 1866), the 1797 Restriction Act that made it possible for the Bank of England to issue bank notes without gold backing, the 1867 Reform Bill that expanded the franchise to those without property, and the 1861 repeal of paper duties that allowed for a greater circulation of mass publications and currency, Poovey admits the influence of empire on Victorian literature of credit,[16] arguing that the Victorian novel was the first to put representation on the line because finance troubles symbolic codes and authority. Poovey herself does not directly address questions of empire, referring instead in a footnote to H. V. Bowen's *The Business of Empire: The East India Company and Imperial Britain*, which does mention the work of novels but only their role in transporting information about the colonies back to the British metropolis.[17] Goodlad's analysis, on the other hand, elaborates the relationship of Victorian modernism to empire by focusing on the history of liberalism (in this case, ethical heterogeneity): "Imperialism's spatial disjunction," she writes, "begins much earlier" (30) than modernist critics date it, informing a realist style as early as 1788 that becomes fully vital in 1857 with the Indian Mutiny. As Anna Kornbluh points out, however, Goodlad's account is mostly concerned with treating novels as informational or data driven: "What does a novel bring to the representation of capitalist globalization," Kornbluh asks of Goodlad, "that journalism or corporate handbooks cannot?" ("Realism's Empire" 151). Victorian realism does, says Kornbluh, use metonymical displacements to reveal spatial expansion and "shifting boundaries of Britishness" (152) with a view toward imperial finance.

Such metonymic displacements are already inside of the money form even before physical displacements and spatial expansions become their markers. For "money," I borrow Antonio Negri's definition in *Marx beyond Marx*. Money for Negri comes conceptually before exchange, as an antagonism or a social crisis that is ontological. It is a fiction that masks the exploitation—"*the equivalence of a social inequality*" (Negri 26; original emphasis)—inside of value; that is, money hides the content of concrete inequality within the form of abstract equality, just as Lizzie is unequal to the social position that her money and diamonds allow her to seem equal to.

For Negri, even before exchange, necessity struggles against the abstract market value of the commodity and its surplus,[18] just as Lizzie struggles with the Eustace lawyers over the abstraction of property as it becomes a category of value that excludes her in its universalism. An equalizing legal terminology that ought to have depersonalized and abstracted possession in order to include those like Lizzie butts heads against the unworthiness of Lizzie's claim to ownership and sameness. Undeserving, Lizzie, we are told, is just acting or lying. As Negri understands money as irreducible to its representation in universal exchange—that is, as "*the primary practical antagonism within whatever categorical foundation*" (23)—we see in Lizzie an acknowledgment of unacknowledged inequality. As much as Poovey understands conventions of imaginative writing as emergent at a certain time when money needed to have its users believe its value as nonimaginative,[19] *The Eustace Diamonds* displays the belief in money's realism and universalism as troubled by Lizzie's possession of it. Trollope loves money (as the exemplar of sympathy and abstract universalizing value and so of his own narrative technique) as much as he faults Lizzie for having it.

Leading up to the Peel Banking Act of 1844, when the central bank in London started to have exclusive control over monetary policy in England and the issuance of paper money over coin, realist form developed inside of a money economy based on financial objects: paper, with its absence of metals, and debt, a circulating amount without footing in bankable reserves. In many ways, the Victorians were obsessed with the imaginary of money and its excess of value against an assumed quantifiable value expressed in material forms and objects.[20] For example, in his classic book *Lombard Street*, founding editor of *The Economist* Walter Bagehot warns of the disaster that would befall the Bank of England if all "our debts payable on demand" (30) were actually demanded, since the reserves could not meet them. Kornbluh remarks that such seeming distrust of the fictional quality of money that critics have noted actually belies an acknowledgment and acceptance: "*They simply acted as if it did not matter that everyone knew that capital values were imaginary*" (*Realizing Capital* 8–9). The metaphysical question of capital's groundlessness, Kornbluh continues, is resolved in the development of capital as a character—through the birth of psychology, for example, the idea of a psychic economy that pervades psychoanalysis or the prevalence of insecure or unstable economic actors in panic.[21]

But what would happen to the realist character if the irresolution of capitalist fictional value *were* the character of capitalist value and could not be resolved psychologically—because money could not extricate itself completely from imaginative writing? In the wake of the 1866 crisis that saw runs on banks and that made the major discount bank Overend, Gurney, and Co. fail, *The Eustace Diamonds* considers Lizzie's character, unable to pay her debts, as an example of just such financial falseness. The debates over the diamonds are irreconcilable with the known categories of property: they are an objective, identifiable representation of immaterial, floating, indeterminable value, both incredibly solid and unquestionably imaginary. The diamonds are deceptive because all language is deficient, but particularly when it is intentionally false, or fictional. As I show in the next section, capital's fictitiousness and resultant cognitive uncertainty occasion at least partly from the diamonds' connection to imperial speculation. Evoking imaginary lands beyond the territorial boundaries of England, the diamonds—with their ornamental, exotic, mystical, and aesthetic qualities that Trollope hates—are excessive to their objective form as determined in the realist language of English law.[22]

As Poovey has documented, before the disciplines of literature and political economy were sharply distinguished through the historical emergence of a "fact/fiction continuum," the tools of imaginative writing developed in literary practice—processes of evaluation and prediction, for example—were used as well to foster credibility in credit and neutralize monetary instruments (*Modern Fact*). Authors such as Charles Dickens were writing popular articles on economics including recommendations to Parliament, building corrupt criminal characters that infused lies into balance sheets. The very creation of the "invisible hand" as a concept grew alongside the development of literary "character" as an abstract actor in an imagined social world. When Henry Sidgwick asked the question "What Is Money?" in the *Fortnightly Review* (which had also published *The Eustace Diamonds* serially), he explained to the unaware British public that credit was the extension of coin and paper beyond the limits of their material forms and created the conditions of Britain's imperial strength and prosperity as debt; he may here have been responding to Dickens. Dickens asked the same question thirty years prior in his 1848 novel *Dombey and Son*, which posed the limits of finance capital in moral indebtedness: love, charity, duty, and eternal life. "What is money after all?" inquires the Dombey son Paul. "If it's a good thing, and can do anything . . . , I wonder why it didn't save me my Mama" (Dickens 99), and then Paul himself cannot be saved from sickness. Sidgwick claimed that, contra Dombey, money does transcend its material presence as a type of sympathetic fictional spirit.

The connection between fiction and finance could go either of two ways: money could be thought of as essentially like fiction—therefore always potentially losing value and needing theoretical modes to distinguish when to trust or not to trust its claim on value—or money could be thought of as always in danger of being counterfeited by "a few bad apples" or people of malicious intent. Lizzie's character—like Lucy's "truth"—intersects these two possibilities. Though in the eighteenth-century monetary value was anchored in reference to the "intrinsick value" of tokens of exchange (Poovey, *Genres* 58), finance was still rife with dangerous, roving fictions like Lizzie. Daniel Defoe, for instance, who is attributed with the first formulation of what would become the British novel in *Robinson Crusoe*, a book that actively denied its own fictionality,[23] also penned a tract that appeared in 1719, entitled "The Anatomy of Exchange Alley; or, A System of Stock-Jobbing."

In this tract, Defoe rails against those spreaders of fictional tales, rumors, and lies who create bubbles in stock prices. Even though "every kind of monetary token also relied on some kind of writing to enable it to serve the . . . functions that money had to perform," comments Poovey, "as various forms of paper were increasingly used to address the scarcity of coins, the theoretical problem presented by all forms of representative money became increasingly clear" (*Genres* 59). Money is a problem because its deception is not always intentional but may be inherent in representational forms.

Even after we have entered a domain governed by the "fact/fiction continuum," which Poovey places in the early nineteenth century (though she finds traces of it back through the seventeenth), practitioners continued to use fiction pedagogically in order to make economic theory accessible to a broader public. Fiction could teach nonpractitioners to think of markets and money in moral terms and might also extract moral character in relation to the money form. Banker George Rae, in his 1885 "Testimony of a Balance-Sheet," for example, displays the balance sheet as the outer representation of a man's concealed inner moral character. As a conventionalized, official form that might still cover deceptive details with abstractions, columns, and numbers, balance sheets unbalance representation itself. Balance sheets might "decoy" you by a "spurious" "lure" (Rae 25), asset declarations and values might be corrupted, liabilities might be subject to contingencies, ships might sink at sea. We learn that the subjectivity of the modern man of business is excessive to the terms of its representation and always potentially dangerously fictional due to the uncertainties behind quantitative conventions; also, we learn that the balance sheet is an instrument for character construction and that it is subject, in some sense, to linguistic laws of abstraction and signification.

Poovey argues that the "problem of representation" for money became visible at times of crisis.[24] The lack of solidity of value was met with attempts to master it in rationalized representations—coins, currency, contracts, and concessions—that failed.[25] Victorians were trying to figure out and gain control of an economy where the "intrinsick value" in things was antagonized by its own moving representations.[26] One year after the publication of *David Copperfield*, in 1851, Sidney Laman Blanchard, for example, writes "A Biography of a Bad Shilling," where a coin (like David) tells a self-conscious story of his own birth, life adventures, and eventual discovery and demise. This financial persona, or metal, circulates through various exchanges and has feelings, sympathies, and moral judgments in crisp, erudite prose, all along teaching the reader how finance works. The coin is faceless and cosmopolitan, fitting in socially with other pocketed objects, sometimes as their equal.[27] He is a perennial sympathetic subject, able to feel along with his fellow coins in whatever environment or situation they encounter and to take on their pain, combining their interests with his own. His voice is one of abstract and objective observation as he comes to express, like realism or the Trollopian narrator, a Lukacian social totality.[28] He makes clear that his tradable value depends on the artistic expertise—the counterfeiter—that made him worth more than he appeared. Like Lizzie Eustace, because of his falseness, the coin adopts the guise of abstract equality, comfortable in a smelly fortress where fake coins were minted or in an ill-ventilated working-class domicile as much as in the hands of a tobacconist or a department store manager or in a court of law.[29] Because of his sympathies—his "we"-ness—the coin raises the question of when his falseness is another name for a legitimate creation of value, and therefore he is identical with the other coins, or when it is intentionally deceptive. In the end, the coin is discovered and nailed to the cross.

*The Eustace Diamonds* similarly revels in money's ability to accumulate and represent value for the Eustace heir through the diamonds' circulation and displacements. It worries over where the diamonds go, as if in a hat trick, and if the law can control their value, just as it worries over Lizzie's lies. Nineteenth-century financiers still had to convince the public to trust in money by directly lauding economic fictions as the key to national prosperity. As Walter Bagehot pronounced, "There is no country at present, and there never was any country before, in which the ratio of the cash reserve to the bank deposits was so small as it is now in England" (18), and such a ratio, Henry Sidgwick clarified in his critique, makes the banking system that fuels the empire fragile and also infallible.

## DEBT

The 1857 Indian Mutiny exposed what Jenny Sharpe has called a "crisis in British authority" (4)—the lie behind the legitimacy of Britain's hold on empire. Though Sharpe is concerned with the rise of false reports about sexual assaults of native men on white women in India, anxieties about the fictionality behind Britain's financial ascendency through fictional money and debt might likewise be said to expose "a British failure to command authority" (87), where the certainties of supremacy and domination might be disclosed as but an empty shell. In fact, in *The Moonstone*, Wilkie Collins's 1868 sensationalist detective novel—often considered "the first" detective novel—on which Trollope bases the plot of *The Eustace Diamonds* (despite Trollope's well-known distaste for sensationalist literature), the diamonds are stolen from an Indian temple in Mysore at the tail end of the Indian Mutiny, and their British inheritors cannot keep hold of them: no matter what security British banks offer to the diamonds, the Indians steal them back, seemingly with the help of ritualistic magic. Where the excess of value in *The Moonstone*'s diamonds emanates from their provenance in a mystical Hindu religion, the excess of spirit and value in the Eustace diamonds is borrowed directly from finance.

As a rewritten plot, *The Eustace Diamonds* is also borrowed on credit, a plot of questionable parentage, name, authority, and possession. Likewise putting under scrutiny how fictional property can be owned, Lizzie Eustace's insistence that the diamonds are hers despite the counterclaims of the Eustace estate after her husband's death suggests that authority, authorship, and possession are not necessarily in the hands of the people to whom they should belong according to the traditions of the social order, just as sovereign authority might be wrested from its "rightful" domain, in *The Moonstone*, with a curse. In a similar vein, Trollope's 1858 novel *Doctor Thorne* tells how an established land-owning family, the Greshams, fall increasingly in debt to the industrial stonemason and lowly railway magnate Roger Scatcherd and his son, who eventually acquire their lands, their houses, and their parliamentary seat and even aspire to woo the son's intended wife, despite the Scatcherds' "intrinsick" tendencies to debauchery, vulgarity, and other bad conduct. The shifting character of the diamonds in *The Eustace Diamonds* suggests that their authority—as fiction—could be transferred, leveraged, speculated, renamed, and illegitimately seized by the likes of Scatcherd or Hindu mystics or Lizzie, just like money.

Though authors like Deborah James argue that in post-Apartheid South Africa, "debt was justified . . . having enabled the expansion of . . . [the] middle class" (4) because "new opportunities for credit were suddenly made available" (4), the question of debt, in the late nineteenth century as in the late twentieth, is not all about acquiring purchasing power, as the Scatcherd case demonstrates. Debt foregrounds issues of control, sovereignty, hierarchy, and who gets to decide on the future as these issues play out in a class society. It also foregrounds issues of how the future will be lived. Nineteenth-century fiction like *The Eustace Diamonds* and *Doctor Thorne* intimates what will become a twentieth- and twenty-first-century reality—that debt has replaced armies for imperial control. Though what Goodlad calls the "heirloom establishment" (100) of parliamentary politics does not seemingly dominate *The Eustace Diamonds* as it does the other Palliser novels,[30] on the novel's margins, a parliamentary debate does ensue about the fate of an Indian prince, the Sawab, in the wake of the Indian Mutiny. A rendition of a historical incident in Mysore, the Sawab wants his adopted son to replace him on the throne while the liberals in power want, instead, to annex the region and rule directly by extending a "free trade" policy.[31] The debate in Parliament in *The Eustace Diamonds* poses liberals such as Fawn, who believe in imperial expansion through annexation in "free trade policies," against Tories such as Greystock, who, though out of majority power, seeks to establish traditional princedoms loyal to Britain that would rule through ritual displays of power.[32] Fawn's and Greystock's contrasting positions vis-à-vis British rule reflect their opposing views on Lizzie and the diamonds. These marginal parliamentary allusions are much more central than they seem.

According to Goodlad, Trollope was "at best ambivalent" (87) about British dominion in India even as he supported British territorial expansion through settlement in places like Canada, Australia, Ireland, and the West Indies, where he thought the indigenous populations would die out. As with the diamonds, the question of the Sawab's claims is a question of legal representation, whether his principality is like a British "heirloom," an object that can be handed down through generations, or a false claim like Lizzie's or Scatcherd's, with his adopted son a usurper of power. The parliamentary question circled around whether British law can be sympathetic to Indian claims—whether, that is, like the narrator of *The Eustace Diamonds*, British law can imaginatively share fellow feeling with its Indian subjects or whether, like Lizzie (maybe), the Sawab was an intentional counterfeit, a fraud, as the Conservatives professed. Lizzie's betrothed, the somewhat incompetent and weak liberal Lord Fawn, expresses the liberal line when writing to Lizzie, begging her to release him from his ill-considered engagement: he had, he laments, encouraged her "to place the diamonds in neutral hands" just as, he thinks to himself, he "was often called upon to be neutral in reference to the condition of outlying Indian principalities" (Trollope, *Eustace* 647). Lord Fawn recognizes the similar legal error in the Sawab's sovereign claims for his princedom and

Lizzie's for the diamonds, declaring, "As far as I can see, lawyers always are wrong. About those nine lacs of rupees for the Sawab, Finlay was all wrong. Camperdown [the Eustace lawyer] owns that he was wrong. If, after all, the diamonds were hers, I'm sure I don't know what I am to do" (547–48). As debt, Lizzie's imposture grants her a right to possession of the diamonds (and therefore to belong to the propertied classes) that is simultaneously legitimate and illegitimate. The Indian prince's claim to a right of sovereign power over British heirloom possessions is similar, based on the claim that he is "like" the British by imitating British "heirloom" elite power and advancing their power interests in the name of "free trade."[33]

An abstract, universalizing right to property, on which liberal trade policies and the expansion of commercial power should rely, would be incompatible with a type of property ownership that, like the "heirloom," assumes and reinforces exclusivity and inequalities. As with the debate in the United States over whether Puerto Ricans could be assimilated into American citizenship, the British parliamentary Conservative idea (represented by Frank Greystock) was that the Indian Mutiny proved India to be unassimilable to capitalist governance—they were, like Lizzie but because of race, exceptional: not fit for either inheriting the "heirloom" of British culture or adapting to the dominion of commodities. "On neither side," Trollope tells us, "did the hearers care much for the Sawab's claims" (*Eustace* 99). There is no sympathy here—that is, no legal or economic narrative framework in which "fellow feeling" with the Sawab could build into a sharing of interests. Such blocking of sympathetic feeling in legislating imperial possession distinguishes the moral fabric of the British character, what gives it authority. An example of Lucy's being "good as gold" is in her attitude toward the Sawab—she reads Frank's speech and decides to take the Sawab's side. In response, the narrator judges her as possessing "a great power of sympathy" (98). Yet even "good as gold," Lucy is unsure if her sympathies really lie with the Sawab or, romantically, with Frank. Is Lucy really so very true?

In the plot of the Sawab, *The Eustace Diamonds* makes clear that decisions over the management of the empire are fashioned according to a logic of financialization. Simultaneously with its debates over the Sawab's fate and the extension of Britain's sovereign representation, the Parliament is deciding in what sense the Bank of England should control representation of its credit lines in coin. Mr. Palliser, a liberal member of Parliament (who in a later novel becomes prime minister), wants to increase the value of the penny, despite its weight in metal, and add in the value of two farthings. A comical discussion ensues (and Trollope is not known for his sense of humor) as to what might happen to a coin whose name referenced a value higher than its worth—that is, if the coin itself, like the diamonds and the Sawab, owed a debt. The coin is counterfeit, intentionally counterfeit, but still official and true, so representation of value itself becomes a means of dispossession.

## CONCLUSION

The conclusion is predictable: Frank Greystock marries Lucy Morris, and Lizzie ends up marrying (predictably) a Jewish preacher, Mr. Emilius, an equally hated, greasy imposter, in her own class, who in a later novel is discarded as a bigamist and a murderer. Once in the hands of the robbers, either the necklace "was to be proved" (749) in the hands of a Russian princess according to the lawyers or, more likely, as the police believed (like modern-day debts as derivatives), its diamonds were cut up and sold on the continent, as was predicted but never occurred in *The Moonstone*, where the diamonds stayed intact as ritualistic objects. Outside of the Eustace sphere, the diamonds had greater value as exchange objects than as ornamental pieces embellishing the domestic establishments and status of the great names or as sacred religious pieces around which rituals were performed. Afterward, the narrator leaves off trying to tell us whose diamonds and what sort of property they were, abandoning this main thread of the novel's discourse—just as he abandoned telling us about the Sawab's fate or Greystock's speech.

Annie McClanahan faults the nineteenth-century realist novel for teaching people to accept the vicissitudes of the credit-based economy and humanizing its effects through narrative closures. "Literary representations of credit," she writes, "likewise reassure economic actors that the social relationships on which the credit contract depends are equitable and stable" (2). On the other hand, she continues, twenty-first-century credit narratives, like horror movies, refuse "to comfort or humanize . . . because the credibility that a few hundred years of capitalist ideology sought to render self-evident has suddenly dissolved" (3). Yet, as with the Sawab's sovereign claims, the narrative of *The Eustace Diamonds* does not close down the diamonds' meanings inside of an "heirloom" status—in opposition to heirlooms, the diamonds are constantly reset and revalued. The novel still posits a possible success for Lizzie's attempt at class annulment that might have succeeded, even when (or especially when) the box is empty, and a warning that we—meaning a class of readers of literature or possessors of money—should all, even as we indulge in such fictions, still fear fictions like hers.

The Victorian realist novel creates characters whose lives and situations are caught in the contradictions of money as equal exchangeable representation in a context of deep social inequalities. *The Eustace Diamonds* was particularly concerned with how money, as a financial system of nonreferential representation based on abstract universal equivalents and future promise, could still confer real value in the present, but it did not settle the matter. At the same time as it reflected on its unfamiliar culture of money, the US Congress of the late nineteenth century was preventing Puerto Rico from receiving political representation equal to states and from being brought under the legal umbrella of equal citizenship. Without the assurance of self-determination and property rights conferred on US citizens, Puerto Rican institutions could be sold off to make up for the "loss of earnings" that could not be earned without those property rights, basically mortgaging its future to be authoritatively controlled by others while it remained perennially and essentially in debt. This is surely the fate of the Sawab, who could not get Parliament to recognize his sovereign rights to govern, and of Lizzie as well. In a sense, through Lizzie's character of class aspirant and imposture, *The Eustace Diamonds* suggests that everyone is in debt because the equal value that money promises in its representations and abstract calculations is always, like a lyric, false in its present, like Parliament's penny. Trollope opens the question of how value is represented when it does not exist in a thing and how to tell the difference between such financial representations' fiction and fact. He does not resolve this.

What the twenty-first century teaches us is to see that the lie was not Lizzie's to begin with. While Trollope gives Lizzie the lie in order to finally punish her for it, Eustace sacrifices Lizzie to debt. Dying, Eustace is the one who lays the lie on Lizzie, clasping it around her neck as the visibly defining signature of her difference: her fakeness, her unworthiness and moral failing, and her nothingness, justifying the hatred directed toward her by the author, the narrator, and the other characters. Defending the rest of the Eustace class from the scarlet letter of fictional value, Lizzie's debt is the form taken by the surplus that they need to make them dazzle, the surplus or supplement that they can profit from by disparaging, dispossessing, resisting, and undervaluing it on her. By fooling the police and almost willingly getting rid of the diamonds, Lizzie might be seen to be, for a moment, refusing the control of "heirloom" authority or the flattening of time—where the future is sold off in the present—that Maurizio Lazzarato posits as debt's life and fallout. Yet to be written is a critical reading of *The Eustace Diamonds* that would *commend* Lizzie—with her indebtedness, her stubbornness, her lies and resistant fictions—as not an antihero but a hero for using the symbols of privilege against themselves and thereby confusing the rituals that uphold wealth and ruling-class authority or, better yet, a reading where her indebtedness would create the conditions that could overcome social and political control through debt.

# CHAPTER 2

## DEBT'S GEOGRAPHIES

*Inequality, or Development's Dance with Dead Capital*

> It had become his business to get up the subject, and then discuss with his principal, Lord Cantrip, the expediency of advising the Government to lend a company five million of money, in order that this railway might be made. It was a big subject, and the contemplation of it gratified him. It required that he should look forward to great events, and exercise the wisdom of a statesman. What was the chance of these colonies being swallowed up by those other regions,—once colonies,—of which the map that hung in the corner told so eloquent a tale? And if so, would the five million ever be repaid? And if not swallowed up, were the colonies worth so great an adventure of national money? Could they repay it? Would they do so? Should they be made to do so?
>
> —Anthony Trollope, *Phineas Finn* (160)

This chapter traces a "Third World" narrative of debt. The previous chapter investigated literature's involvement in creating a belief in *something not there* that had value for the incipient world of finance; the financialization of the "Third World" also requires a set of abstractions, borrowing from literature, where the narrative object of debt appears as "*something else*" (Clover, "Autumn" 45) and as *somewhere else*. In fact, it might be said that the "Third

World" comes into appearance as such a negative category of representation—a "Third World"—through a sort of debt where the object that *is not there* gets transposed onto a space of negative difference. This chapter argues, therefore, that literature creates a "Third World" identity as fictional in modes that parallel debt as fictional value.

The choice of the term *Third World* is very deliberate here—I don't intend it to refer to a nonaligned Cold War entity subordinated to a conflict between superpowers or a pretechnological region playing catchup in a world of technological progress, though I realize that those types of meanings have been granted to the term historically and criticized appropriately as monological, racist, primitivist, and supremacist. Rather, what I mean by "Third World" is a particular structural position within the geopolitical globe that, in a world systems sense and because of its continued disempowerment through histories of colonial and other geopolitical subordinating relationships, is vulnerable to exploitation in current schemes of economic accumulation. As such, "Third World" does not exist in any other form but by its fictional usage, and yet it allows for global power relations to be seen as having similar effects in multiple sites—effects worth thinking about in their similarities even as they interact with different local cultures. Because of its history, the "Third World" carries activist claims, sympathies, and coalitions, as well as a critique of the normative economic order.[1] As Ella Shohat remarks, "The term 'Third World' contains a common project of linked resistances to neo-colonialisms. Within the North American context, more specifically, it has become a term of empowerment for inter-communal coalitions of various peoples of color" (111).

This chapter moves from Nobel Prize–winning Nigerian playwright Wole Soyinka's 1965 play *The Road* to celebrated Kenyan novelist Ngugi wa Thiong'o's 2006 novel *Wizard of the Crow*, detailing how neoliberalism inserts its logics inside the ideologies that debt produces. *The Road* tells of drivers who profit by selling dead people's possessions after road accidents—the living need to borrow from death in order to live, as, for Marx, living labor is enthralled to dead capital, and they then "owe" time back to the gods as work. *Wizard of the Crow* is a comedy of errors telling of a fictional "Third World" nation with the name Aburiria[2] whose entire state apparatus is wrapped up in debt as the Ruler's sovereignty is financed out to foreign investors. As, in its metaphysical logic, *The Road* locates the ideology of debt in the relationship between commodities and gods of the dead, *Wizard of the Crow* is about antiproduction:[3] the displacement of the worker and the commodity, the breakdown of the machine, the destruction of its made world, the death of the social.

*Wizard of the Crow* foregrounds a very basic problematic in the relationship between neoliberalism and economies of debt. Liberalism envisions debt as part of a contract. In classical liberalism, the contract is assumed to be political between citizens and states, where the citizen gives up its freedom in exchange for security. This configuration of the contract translates into an economic arrangement: equal parties enter into an agreement where something is handed over from one to the other with the understanding of an eventual return. If a rich nation or bank grants a loan to a "Third World" country, the idea behind it should be that the money will be used to build up productive infrastructure that would enable the debtor to pay back the debt even while expanding economic potential. However, debt is instead an agreement between unequal partners or, as *Wizard* foregrounds, a situation where the partners are so unequal that the contract is forced by one party onto another for the benefit of only one side. Neoliberal debt restructuring has required debtor countries to divest from developmental initiatives and infrastructure, thereby reducing or even destroying the productive capacities of the "Third World" country to deliver on the debt. Debt under neoliberalism is therefore in the service of power, destroying cultures by destroying work and workers' lives. *Wizard* demonstrates this nexus between increasing debt and the shrinking credibility of the promise of the material world.

*Wizard* emphasizes literature's place in exhibiting this destruction of the material world enacted through debt because it brings up the question of who controls the relationship between languages and realities. Remember that the story of Babel is also a story about the potential to challenge God the creator by giving humans language—building, diversifying, and extending language and its power to signify, to create worlds of meaning in competition with supreme power. But the project fails. As soon as the Ruler and his cronies start negotiations for the grand construction project of the Tower (or even before), the coherence of the territory, the state, the economy, and the literary trajectory all come apart simultaneously. The streets in the business zone are filled with "flies, worms, and the stench of rot" (Ngugi, *Wizard* 36) caused by "mountains of uncollected garbage, the factories in the industrial area, or simply from human sweat" (48), and Kamiti, soon to be the Wizard, detaches in spirit form from this territory and from his working body due to hunger and unemployment, "the wounds of fruitless quests" (47). National industry here is reduced to excreting death, and labor is immersed in the waste of past production, with no employment openings available even for cleaning toilets: "Are there any toilets left . . . ?" (51). Here the instruments of production make waste, death, and rot and as such are disconnected from living processes, and the machine does not need the worker even for accumulating more shit.

This death of production affects even the creative powers of language: "no vacancy" publicizes the situation of worker obsolescence while at the same time explaining that language can no longer *do its work* in an antiproductive, dead region. For example, Tajirika (soon to be in charge of the Tower project and then to be the future Ruler) questions Kamiti's use of modern English, particularly his ability to read, understand, and interpret the sign "*No Vacancy*" (59). Tajirika reminds Kamiti that, as the East India

Company's control has been handed over to the modern construction and real estate company for which he works, the standards of acceptable English since the seventeenth century, which he learned during colonization, are no longer relevant. Whereas meaning-making had been grounded in old forms of slavery, conquest, and domination, it was now grounded in new forms of exploitation, most prevalently debt (negative value, or waste). The destruction of standard literary English and the destruction of national production are thereby linked.

*The Road* is a story about the relationship between dead capital and living labor on the road to progress in a floundering developing state. The state comes across as comical in the form of the Professor with out-of-place habits who preaches spiritualism in the Word while turned away from those in his immediate service, an absurd idealist with his eyes to the sky. Dressed in Victorian tails and bearing old newspapers and garbage, the Professor comes on stage bearing a sign that says "BEND" that he stole from off the road. "BEND" is a spiritual descriptor of the road—the material apparatus underlying productive motion and progress. Once the sign is removed from the road, commuters no longer are certain of their way—they roll straight forward, toward death. The sign "BEND" divides living labor from dead capital—those workers inside the productive machine, licensed to work by the Professor (who issues counterfeit work licenses for a fee), from those bodies piled up by the side of the road. The mythological spirit of death, Ogun, dances around the players in a mask. The Professor oversees the collection of commodities from the strewn bodies on the road and resells them, so their dead bodies are the machines of profit. The word "BEND" thus pivots, opening up a spiritual communication with the gods as a sign of technological advancement, development, and rising worker well-being—or reproduction—which its removal closes down in sacrifice and death. *The Road* raises the question of the corrupt misappropriation of the sign of progress, a misappropriation that stymies development with its hopes and promises.

Reading *The Road* and *Wizard of the Crow* together—two works that take up debt in its relationship to colonialism—reveals that neoliberalism intensifies the postcolonial capture of dead capital through debt by sacrificing productive living economies of the commodity. Each work takes up the narrative of a development project—the road in *The Road* and the Tower in *Wizard*—as the physical form of power, but the relation of the project to the space of development is different in each case. In *Wizard*, the Tower is a false promise, never to materialize and so alienating the possibilities offered by controlling the material construction of meaning. Though *Wizard* is steeped in mythological and religious codes, as the centrality of the Tower of Babel would suggest, the idea of transcendence or material transformation that the biblical Tower might offer in the word of God has no possibility of connecting with the situation described for "Third World" citizens on the ground—it is, in fact, comic. In contrast, with the road open to death-inducing corruption and appropriation, *The Road* is concerned with a metaphysics of debt, where the inequalities that seem steeped in religious ritual second as identities politicized in relation to the postcolony. Whereas in *The Road*, debt reignites tradition, local culture, rituals, and relations with the gods to merge with modern work-related inequalities and techniques of dispossession, in *Wizard*, debt has the power to transform culture in its totality by replacing work. The two texts also recognize that debt's territorial alienations, where the ends of finance are to turn profits *somewhere else*, are caught in a similar relationship to that which the literary word has with the object of its representation. *The Road* shows the postcolonial elite and the workers struggling over the power to signify, while *Wizard* displays signification as disassociated from the needs and concerns of the national body as it, like finance, turns toward geopolitical power centers and away from communities, commodities, and productive employment.

## SYMBOLIC EXCHANGE

Literary scholarship has taken account of financialization's encounters with "Third World" narratives, but not debt per se. Alison Shonkwiler uses the word *financial* rather than "*neoliberal*" or *postcolonial* because *financial* exposes the "process of creating value" (xxviii), securing abstract value in real things by securing imaginary power relations as real. This insight certainly applies to *Wizard of the Crow*, where the Tower never exists except as an unlikely plan and a vulture fund, as it only serves to gouge the economic base: financial power seeks to surrender all social relations before its own version of imaginary social relations. Most famously, Ian Baucom, citing Arrighi, notes the importance of the realist novel's character typologies for the forms of risk and insurance adjustments fueling the Atlantic slave trade in the eighteenth and nineteenth centuries. The protagonist in the realist novel is a quantity, an accumulation of experience and adventure that turns into a "type," or an object identifiable within a range of social positions. Like the English novel, the practice of insurance invents an "average" type and situation based in similar generalized abstractions. According to Baucom, insurance and its calculations of risk, like the novel, require that "the particular object which it considers and which it has placed within its determinate moment, is, to some extent, typical of that moment" and that "the situation itself will then be taken (at least in part) to define the objects it circumscribes" (44). Ericka Beckman likewise notices how "novels highlight finance capital as an illusory and indeed fictive form of wealth" (97) in late nineteenth- through twentieth-century literary narratives. Latin American financial narratives, she says, register economic imbalances showing the psychological damage done by the failure of the economy to sustain equivalences between these characters and their commodity contexts. The system of equivalences will "fail to accurately represent value, leading to all kinds of disruptions and short-circuits in exchange" (85) that reflect in the characters' psychologies. For Beckman, these failures are often personal and subjective, marked by nervous and psychological crises.[4] Beckman acknowledges that money's abstractions are constituted intentionally as unstable, even failing, by imposing inequalities of the creditor-debtor relationship into the structure of character.

Much of this new scholarship on literature and finance has followed Derrida in addressing literature's role in producing equivalencies in value that tend toward balance, even if precariously, or at least suggest that catharsis would lead toward equilibrium rather than projecting disequilibrium as, ultimately, the norm. In line with deconstruction's reliance on structural linguistics, which understands signifiers of meaning to be referring to other signifiers of meaning, such criticism generally envisions symbolic exchange, similarly to ideologies of market exchange, as operating within a system of made equivalencies in language: "What must be interrogated, it seems," explains Derrida in his analysis of the gift, "is precisely this being-together, the at-the-same-time, the synthesis, the symmetry, the syntax, or the system, the *syn* that joins together two processes as incompatible as that of the gift and that of exchange" (37–38). This partial story does not take into account Bakhtin's analysis of the centrifugal forces that tie literature to its social milieu, its expression of disequilibrium and distance,[5] the impasse in the exchange between the call to alliance and the body-to-be-allied.[6] Whereas Derrida's analysis is based on de-emphasizing and dismantling the essential differences between a gift and an exchange, as both need to be answered with an equal but impossible return, debt triggers types of narrative that extend indefinitely the time in which returns are not returned because the indebted are denied access to the means of return, making them unequal to the exchange.[7]

This chapter argues that adding the "Third World" into the mix undoes the ideology of exchange through equivalence. If, as Derrida proposes, the system of equivalencies is based on the erasure of the object of signification (e.g., the signified), then the "Third World" is that object—the irreconcilable nonequivalent (or indebtedness) in the exchange that calls out the lie in the system. Though for Derrida, every empirical object is erased in the signifying economy of exchange so that symbolic equivalence empties the materiality of human suffering of its distinct importance and ethical claims, Theodor Adorno, in contrast, poses human suffering as an actuality that disrupts subjective comfort and accommodations of the subject within the objective world. As Adorno declares, "Suffering remains foreign to knowledge; though knowledge can subordinate it conceptually and provide means for its amelioration, knowledge can scarcely express it through its own means of experience without itself becoming irrational" (18).[8]

The "Third World" has a privileged relation to Derridian aporias, the remainder that symbolization cannot equalize, because of its history as the victim of organized expropriation. The history of the "Third World" attests that the system of exchange was never an outcome of equivalencies but instead constructed on top of radical inequalities hidden under the appearances of equality. A "Third World" literature of debt, then, would show how literature's role in producing representations of objects referring to other representations of objects to create equal value breaks down in the context of global exchange. Foregrounding the destruction of real and potential productive capacities, a "Third World" narrative of debt shows the "Third World" as an object that has been displaced, destabilized, or disappeared: its tendency not to conform to symbolic exchange in equal representation dovetails with the reality that it has been coerced into its circuits of exchange on unequal footing.

One important element of such "Third World" literatures of debt is a critical temporality.[9] As Joshua Clover remarks, this aspect of financialization colonizes future time "as if it were space" ("Autumn" 45),[10] ensuring "that all profit is realized finally through the disequilibrium between geographical regions" (42). As Clover adds, "The apparent M-M′ situation of financialization . . . is thus characterized by *the subtraction of time*" (ibid.), meaning that the worth of M′ is simultaneous to M because the change of profit occurs across geographical space. Just as Marx described capital as the struggle over the time of the working day, neoliberalism can be described as a struggle for the domination of geographical space as a method of gaining time. In fact, neoliberalism can be said to expand the distance between regions that spend time in production (where time is subtracted) from regions that take time in profits.

Financialization demands different narrative structures than commodity culture because it no longer relies on progressive accumulation in object production but rather on an avoidance of objects that decelerate the speed of accumulation with stoppages, transportation, breakdowns, conflicts, and the limits of worker productivities. Clover here follows Giovanni Arrighi, who understands Marx's profit formula M-M′ (money gets more money, as in finance) as always in the process of overcoming M-C-M′, or profit through commodity production, progress through the object. The tendency of history, says Arrighi, is to move away from the commodity because it slows down the flow of profit. For example, financial profiteering depends on the destruction of the state's redistributive capacities—that is, on austerity policies such as cuts to public services like education and health care as well as on the promotion of market-based remedies for all social problems. These techniques speed up the transfer of wealth upward, killing productive capacities by denying workers the means to work and reproduce themselves for the next day of work and the next generation. For Arrighi, capital's preferred push is toward monetary flexibilization, or "phases of financial rebirth and expansion" (6). Just as Derrida's referential object is erased to shore up equivalencies between symbolic representations of meaning, Arrighi's view is that money also tends to crush out the commodity object in order to create abstract equivalencies in finance.

## INEQUALITIES AND THE ACCUMULATION OF DEAD CAPITAL

Literary realism, as critics have observed, is historically imbricated in the development of political economy, money, and the credit economy. Realism does not just teach the tenets of political economy to its reading public; it also performs an epistemological function of creating abstract, imaginative categories of identity or character, general composites of experience or "types" in which a broad range of readers may see themselves reflected. As well, realism builds a critique of representations of value alienated from objects and territories, as discussed in the prior chapter. Such realism, notes Thomas Piketty in *Capital in the Twenty-First Century*, links nineteenth-century literary writing with the twenty-first-century economy, both periods marked by increasing inequalities produced by capital's pressure—outlined by Arrighi—to be always extracting itself from the commodity and its temporalities.

Piketty's main concern is with growing inequality or, rather, with how the twentieth century's wars and Great Depression constituted a time when the ratio between capital (private/industrial/corporate profits) and national income (workers' wages) lessened (because of commodity production, industrialization, and the welfare state) in contrast to most times of history, when that ratio remained more or less constant (workers got a lesser share).[11] Piketty believes that inequality results from a growing disparity in the ratio between dead capital (i.e., past surplus labor, usually stored up in productive machines and infrastructure) and living labor. Throughout most of history, this ratio has been level and constant, but the two world wars and the Depression depleted capital's holdings, reducing its share for the purpose of progress and redevelopment, only to be re-elevated at the end of the twentieth century and into the twenty-first, making the twenty-first more like the nineteenth.

This view of the economy and of the causes of inequality is, in Piketty's own assessment, attributable at least in part to literary form and to realism in particular. Taking on a tone of Socratean irony, perhaps, Piketty tells us not to ask economists to explain the nineteenth century's economic inequality (which we are again experiencing now) but rather to turn to other fields, literature most prominently. "Indeed," he begins, "the distribution of wealth is too important an issue to be left to economists," whereas "film and literature, nineteenth-century novels especially, are full of detailed information about the relative wealth and living standards of different social groups, and especially about the deep structure of inequality" (2).[12] Though Trollope is not directly referenced (Austen and Balzac are the reference points here), Piketty's explanations do describe Trollope's plots, where characters' identities (e.g., their positions in career and marriage ambitions or the likelihood of their receiving invitations to important dinner parties, hunting parties, or country houses) are reflected in the price of their inheritance, income, and assets, while there is very little discussion of where the sums come from and how they are promised. The social world seems stable when characters can be known through their assets, holdings, and annuities. Though in the eighteenth and nineteenth centuries, "money had meaning, and novelists did not fail to exploit it, explore it, and turn it into a literary subject" (Piketty 106), in the twentieth century, such focus ceased, says Piketty: "It is surely no accident that money—at least in the form of specific amounts—virtually disappeared from literature after the shocks of 1914–1945" (109). The evidence Piketty gives for this is Orhan Pamuk's *Snow*, which, even though written at a time of skyrocketing inflation in his native Turkey, does not mention "any specific sums" (109). Piketty attributes the lack of direct reference to monetary sums in *Snow* (as representative of all twentieth- and twenty-first-century literatures) to the evening out of the ratio resulting from the destruction of capital in the two world wars and the Depression as well as investments in the worker via the welfare state, unions, and wages: the ratio of past surplus and machinery to the working wage had decreased, but only for a short historical time.

Surely, as we may learn here, literature is also too important an issue to be left to economists.[13] For example, Piketty notes, a nineteenth-century culture of accumulation links individual character and personality to certain sums that are transparent to moral standing. Characters are often identified, recognized, positioned, and *characterized* through the sum of their annual incomes. "When Honoré de Balzac and Jane Austen wrote their novels at the beginning of the nineteenth century, the nature of wealth was relatively clear to all readers" (113), Piketty explains. "For nineteenth-century novelists and their readers, the relation between capital and annual rent was self-evident" (53–45). Whether or not we believe Piketty's allegations of simplicity in nineteenth-century economies and representations (on the contrary, nineteenth-century texts profess anything but easy and universal comprehension or even coherence), twenty-first-century culture might, rather, detect accumulation appearing in other social forms besides directly in inheritance, family name, or estates—in, for example, urban geographies, nation, class, systems of circulation, and financialized social relations, to follow the example of *Snow*. As the novelist John Lanchester jokes in his nonfiction narrative about the 2008 financial crisis, *I.O.U.*, "The whole idea that a banker looks a borrower in the eye and makes a decision on whether he can trust him came to seem laughably nineteenth century" (74). Nevertheless, we should take seriously Piketty's own allegation that inequality results from European nations' disinvesting from sites of production and that its narrative structures must, in parallel, mobilize symbolic structures that disassociate from industrialization's realisms. Financial capital profits through abstracting value from worlds it destroys by draining productive capacities and taking away not just the surplus but also investments in the reproduction of capital. Piketty's faith in literature's relation to the transparent and direct representation of value cannot account for a regime of financial capital that accumulates value by doing away with its relation to (living) things in the world.

The disconnect between capital and living things (or the social relations of the commodity) in colonial and postcolonial places can indeed find a correspondence in literature, though not in the way that Piketty assumes. Theorists have begun to think about how language—particularly in its literary forms—creates symbolic value by disassociating from commodities and material things. Arjun Appadurai, for example, argues that finance depends on the promissory language of the contract, which is performative in the sense that it creates the conditions that the contract needs in order to come into existence. Appadurai terms this "retro-performativity" (from J. L. Austen and Judith Butler) and compares it to the work of rituals "*bringing about the possibilities that will have led to it*" (87). Derivatives are promissory contracts piled up on each other, each one further away from a direct connection to the asset. Crises like the one in 2008 occur, thinks Appadurai, because the promise has been so far removed from the asset that it runs a risk over "whether or not an agreement will emerge *at all*" (94), whether the offerer will find someone with whom to make a deal or, rather, whether the offer of an agreement will make a market. In addition, Appadurai argues, the logic of the derivative follows the logic of metonymy, where personhood is divided up into traits and potentials that can be combined and bundled up with other contiguous traits and potentials: "It is a logic of dividuation [he borrows this term from Gilles Deleuze], in which personhood rests not in the stable crystallization of body, soul, intention, and affect in a single bodily envelope with a name [or, in Trollope's sense, an inheritance], but in the highly volatile relationship between those substances (flesh, blood, vitality, energy, essence, and effluvia) that are always in the process of interacting and recombining to produce temporary assemblages of sociality, identity, and affect" (112). In Appadurai's view, because finance depends on contracts and is therefore linguistically oriented, it necessarily erodes and transforms the material conditions on which it rests.

Yet the contract works inside of liberalism's assumption of abstract equality, where the negotiating partners are free to decide. Appadurai does not see how language's abilities to divide things up and erode its original references through a series of partial replacements can be appropriated by power as a tool for producing inequalities by destroying and devaluing the value-producing means of others. In contrast to Piketty and to Appadurai, Franco "Bifo" Berardi has described capitalism as a series of steps of disconnection between the body and language/representation leading ultimately to "liquidating both the living body of the planet and the social body" (112): the European financial class no longer has an attachment to territory or its particular lived histories.[14] This "dereferentialization" of capital is prefigured in experiments of Symbolist poetry to forget the referent, as a "semio-economy" of capital allows for symbols of value to generate value in other symbols rather than in things: "As symbolism experimented with the separation of the linguistic signifier from its denotational and referential function, so financial capitalism, after internalizing linguistic potencies, has separated the monetary signifier from its function of denotation and reference to physical goods" (Berardi 19).[15] In twentieth-century poetry, "Bifo" maintains, "signs produce signs without any longer passing through flesh" (17), just as, in Arrighi's scheme, money seeks to make money without passing through physical substance, where its process of accumulation slows down.

At the core, Berardi sees "dereferentialization" as a form of "antiproduction" (destruction) where personal responsibility for capital's effects are seemingly erased—in fact, where the symbols of value can destroy the territories from which they are abstracted and removed. Through debt, Berardi is saying, capital destroys the correspondence between language and reality by destroying reality, setting signification free in its own fictions of value: "The accumulation of abstract value is made possible through the subjection of human beings to debt, and through predation on existing resources. The destruction of the real world starts from this emancipation of valorization from the production of useful things. The emancipation of value from the referent leads to the destruction of the existing world" (104–5). Debt has replaced production as the site of abstraction not because, as with production, exchange value no longer relates to concrete needs but rather because debt destroys the world of real needs. In neoliberal Europe under austerity (and by extension, in the neoliberalized "Third World," though that is not his focus), finance in Berardi's view has been divorced from attachments to the territory of the living. Debt finally realizes what Theodor Adorno predicted of the artwork in a commodity culture, that its symbols are "opposed to the empirical world" (1), a "realized materialism [that] would at the same time be the abolition of materialism" (29), a "manifest annihilation of reality" (31).

## *WIZARD OF THE CROW*

For Marx, "capital is dead labour, that, vampire-like, only lives by sucking living labour, and lives more, the more labour it sucks" (*Capital* 224). The production machine consists of the stored working time of past workers that feeds off the life breath of the living. Marx's gothic descriptions of nineteenth-century industrialization pose a fundamental relation between the living and the dead. The worker transforms organic nature by using up the time of his or her working life in production, handing it over to the machine: "Living labour must seize upon these things and rouse them from their death-sleep, change them from mere possible use-values into real and effective ones" (178).

*Wizard of the Crow* narrates a dismantling of this symbiosis between work and the machine. "Why does needy Africa," asks one of its many narrators, "continue to let its wealth meet the needs of those outside its borders and then follow behind with hands outstretched for a loan of the very wealth it let go?" (681). *Wizard* displays the effects on language and culture of the financialization of the economy or the splitting off of productive investment (reproduction) from the aim of profit, where money has a life of its own away from the lives of things. By *money*, I mean a system of representing value that, because it circulates through the production of things, has traditionally also been expressive of social antagonisms. When this form of money turns away from the production of things, *Wizard* shows, the social is expressed as negative value, or debt. Debt culture inhabits *Wizard* not only as content but also as a reflection of this crisis of representation in literary technique. In line with "Bifo"'s insights, debt writing in *Wizard* severs representational values that circulate through living cultures, bodies, time, working institutions, and politics and replaces them with reified objects or empty, deathlike forms: institutional powerlessness, sovereign vacancy, temporal blockages, valueless money, deteriorating body parts replaced by dead and imported machines, waste, and other types of inorganicity, meaninglessness, and obsolescence. Within the novel's debt culture, former producers are unemployed—called "daemons," after the dead—gathering in lines extending in all directions from the "*No Vacancy*" sign outside the construction company, for miles and miles, without the authorities able to stop new arrivals or disperse the crowd. *Wizard* depicts the growing disparity and distancing between the profit machine and work, where debt's profits do not accumulate in the lifetime or identity of the worker (contra Piketty). As "antiproduction," finance means that capital is accumulating in one place while workers in another place are deprived of identity, of the wage (their share of productive income), and thereby of their participation in the construction of their surrounding reality, meaningfulness, and conditions of life.

This detachment of value production from the living underlies the temporal structure of *Wizard of the Crow*. If, as Mathias Nilges claims, the literary narrative is better at examining the temporality of finance than the instruments that finance has produced to understand its own operations, *Wizard of the Crow* is an exemplary novel for thinking about how temporality is managed in the financialized world. The commodity represented by *C* (commodity), Nilges observes, "which once mediated the process of monetary production and accumulation, has been removed from the equation" (32). With its tendencies to reduce the time of profit extraction (friction) to zero by bypassing the commodity, finance witnesses a "narratological crisis connected to a crisis of temporal epistemology: the future is increasingly drawn into the present" (33). Nilges is particularly concerned with finance's ability to wipe out the utopian edge of the future by erasing the future's radicalism under a nostalgia for the endless repetitions of the past's futures, whereas *Wizard* also plays on foreclosures to the liberal, progressive future's promises of equality. In liberal societies like ours, equality is mostly production's progressive promise, or the promise that jobs or salaries will bring everyone who works hard enough to the same level at some point in the future. Reflecting the temporalities of a debt economy, the present in *Wizard* traps future life in the present's repetitions, just as the Ruler locks his wife in a house where the clocks do not move and where the calendars flip to the same date over and over, where everything—even the clothing—extends eternally the moment of her defiance. The promise is over.

Similarly, the plot itself does not follow a course of development based in a model of accumulation such as in the *bildungsroman*, where the end follows from the beginning as accumulated experience feeds the character's moral and intellectual maturation. Rather, in *Wizard*, the end of the story brackets the beginning, displacing it to another point in the narrative that is uncertain and unmarked, making the productive line of story development all but obsolete, circular, backward, and self-annihilating. (I have followed a similar course in this chapter, putting the later literary work first to limit possible readings of the former, so that the past is already constrained by its future.) The dominance of the end (placed at the beginning) destroys what comes before the end, covering it with a fantastic but ungrounded speculation of what must have happened to ensure this end. The novel opens as the Ruler contracts a sickness of which nobody knows the cause but many speculate.[16] Projected backward in retrospect, five different stories are told of the illness's origins, and each of these simultaneous narrative lines ends up depositing concrete details in the subsequent unfolding of the plot, all five mixing haphazardly as though all were equally true, happening in five different potential time zones that nevertheless impossibly overlap.

With symptoms of body enlargement and lightness, the illness, we learn, may have resulted from the Ruler's anger; the anger is caused because the Global Network News fails to interview him during his trip to New York, an event recounted some 460 pages later. Page 471 announces the cause of the Ruler's neurosis that happens on page 1, whereas that neurosis, as well as serious physical ailments, is the effect of the future unknown, of uncertainty (the effect precedes the cause). In New York, the Ruler's unrelentingly inflating body—"further bodily expansion, lightness of the body, and bellyache" (652)—is examined by medical professionals. "The Ruler's body, now more passive [and massive!] than ever, seemed impossibly light; only the ceiling prevented it from floating away" (650). With national sovereignty literally up in the air,[17] the unemployed population at home consults the supernatural to deal with the overwhelming uncertainties of future time when the institutions are already all but defunct. The Ruler is ineffectual because of his hyperinflation: useless, ungrounded, unproductive accumulated matter. "But what to do about the Ruler's unrelenting inflation?" the narrator asks of the fruitless yet unremitting activity of his doctors. "How to stop it, how to slow it down?"

The Ruler's illness turns out to be a pregnancy, where he gives birth to little Baby D: democracy. Yet this little democracy is not the rule of the people, as its nomenclature might suggest; rather, it is a financial plutocracy: "It is unnatural for money to give birth to money," reflects the Wizard with irritation. "Banks alone know the secret of money producing money. They hide the secret in ledger books and computer screens" (660). Whereas pregnancy usually marks time, this pregnancy is about avoiding time by floating, unbound by things. The placement of the Ruler's pregnancy in the United States implies that the profits from African things are floating away from their imputed origins, disassociated. As Berardi elaborates, "Financial signs have led to a parthenogenesis of value, creating money through money without the generative intervention of physical matter and muscular work" (19). Meanwhile, the productive and reproductive capacities of Aburiria contained in the Ruler's body are growing empty, with the emptiness named "Democracy"—Baby D. The Ruler no longer represents a territory but rather floats, pregnant with an uncertain democracy born outside of the nation, outside of political control, without citizens.

*Wizard of the Crow* is a novel about authoritarianism in a "Third World" nation even while the Ruler's authority is treated as a joke.[18] The authoritarianism is the cover through which the financial project is managed. Yet underneath the Ruler's ruse of authority to keep order as the Tower project is negotiated and planned, the social totality increasingly unravels in disorder. Instead of going to work, the citizens of Aburiria line up in front of offices in queues that go for miles in many directions; police are sent out to stop the rumors that jobs and cash are available[19] that compel people to line up (jobs and cash are unavailable, so the lines are interminable), but the police do not return. An unemployed man's soul flies over the city and lands in a garbage heap, and he is taken for dead; he ends up (as wizard) able to read minds, able to see the future in the present by holding the present up to a mirror. In the fourth book, the Global Bank ends the project of the Tower:

"After reviewing the entire project, the Global Bank did not see any economic benefits to Marching to Heaven. To argue that the project would create jobs, as the Aburirian government had claimed, was a case of outdated Keynesian economics" (485). Since the bank's cancellation of the loan happens during the Ruler's illness, and the illness is how the novel starts, the canceling of the loan can be said to precede the original promise of the advance. The end precedes the beginning; the future is consumed in the present; book 4 occurs before book 1, the beginning is treated as a listing of the past possibilities that the future demands, and the present has been sold off to a false promise. The shifting of the story line's sequencing makes it difficult even to determine if Aburiria exists or has existed at all or if it came to be at the convenience of the loaning body, projecting back what must have happened (as the beginning is projecting back what must have happened to make the Ruler ill) as an afterimage or after its death. As a landed territory, Aburiria functions like the diamonds in *The Eustace Diamonds*—very much there, concrete and touchable inasmuch as it is in the process of disappearing as a physical object, made unreal by its financial representation.

What finance means for *Wizard* is a relinquishing of freedom, where instead of temporality opening up to the unpredictable, the accidental, and the undetermined, the future already captures and determines what might happen next or what happened last or even what happens now—the future happens first, closing down possibility. "He, the Ruler," he wants his wife to believe, "had power, real power over everything including . . . yes . . . Time" (7). Instead of granting trust and confidence in the credibility of the world described in the nation of Aburiria, *Wizard* insists that objects can only be secured as real by future acts, as backward reflections of future time. Like the loan, the Ruler's life is a temporal reversal where his birth origin is established only later by a parliamentary act that flows backward, as though he did not exist before the celebration in book 4:

> Now everybody in the country knew something or other about the Ruler's birthday because, before it was firmly set in the national calendar, the date of his birth and the manner of its celebration had been the subject of a heated debate in Parliament that went on for seven months, seven days, seven hours, and seven minutes, and even then the honorable members could not arrive at a consensus mainly because nobody knew for sure the actual date of the Ruler's birth, and when they failed to break the impasse, the honorable members sent a formal delegation to the very seat of power to seek wise guidance, after which they passed a motion of gratitude to the Ruler for helping the chamber find a solution to a problem that had completely defeated their combined knowledge and experience. (12)

As in the last chapter, the abstract categories of the law here are alienated from the objects to which they are to be applied. The supposedly sovereign, legislative body is without the means to represent to the public the national entity over which it legislates and also without the procedures to set up rules on which to base that communication. Trying to determine its concrete origin through an act of power many years later, legislative sovereign power is lost and useless in its comic attempts to bring temporality to heel in legislative code. The sentence is both too long and too short. It turns to comic precision for temporal specificity while insisting on the vagueness of distinguishing historical markers and dates. Even after Parliament adopts the conventions of decision-making and law-confirming deliberations, the beginning of the sentence contradicts the end of the sentence: the subject "everybody" defined by knowing cannot logically lead into a predicate where knowledge is defeated: knowledge is defeated first. The passage is about the emptiness of symbolization even though historical and political currents are rallying for securing its certainty.[20] Challenging sovereignty and certainty, debt breaks apart the narrative conventions and time that the political regime shares with its citizens even while the Ruler's body is increasingly distorted and unmoored through its contaminations, travels, and distresses.

Critics have remarked on the experimental temporalities of *Wizard*. Simon Gikandi, for example, talks about the novel as "a place where time itself is forced to stop" (98), while Ian Macdonald foregrounds its "destabilizing [of] the linear aggregation of Western time" (59). Generally, the temporal disjunctures are read as significant for incorporating the "local folklore and the rhythms of traditional orature" (57), as Macdonald offers, or, as Robert Colson interprets it, the temporal play points to a "future of the nation, a future beyond authoritarian rule" (134), where spoken stories and rumors from multiple narrators weaken the authoritarian grip.[21] Such analysis has followed Ngugi's own framing of global culture as caught in a conflict between orality and writing, with orality as the site where "different forms of being change into each other" (*Globalectics* 76), composed of a mixture between nature and nurture, environmental, human, mythological, and linguistic interchange. The future of the nation in this case, however, rather than leading beyond authoritarian rule, is trapped by always having to pay back its past. The Ruler is replaced by another ruler just like him and then dies, and the story, we assume, repeats—the Global Bank again offers a loan.[22]

Less critical attention has been paid to the story of debt and its relation to time and representation. Yet the novel undoubtedly lends itself to debt's temporality. "Debt is actually future time" (84), says Berardi—the securing of the future's unknowable enigma with a measurement and a calculation where "you take my (future) time" (84) and therefore "the future is no longer conceived as promise, but as threat" (108). *Wizard* takes the classic form of the realist novel, with the story advancing in stages across a vast social tableau that connects numerous characters across geographical space. Noting nineteenth-century realism's "shift from the diachronic to the synchronic" (*Antinomies* 222), Jameson has attributed to realism a new sense of time that substitutes its linear progressivity with a simultaneity (*Middlemarch* is the main reference point here), where the future is made coterminous with the present (even, as Jameson remarks, if the occurrences of the same moment in different locations do not always adequately correspond), and certainly Ngugi inherits this tradition. The event of the People's Assembly, for example, is cut between the Aburirian capital and a foreign hotel in the United States, where the Ruler is watching the celebration on TV with his foreign doctors, ministers, and ambassadors while recovering from his illness, losing control of his body, his country, and his narrative at the same time even while at a distance. The Ruler's illness is happening before the beginning of the novel and across the sea, where the national opposition to the crisis of the Tower is being shown as news on TV. The Ruler knows himself and his country only as a virtual image captured and mediated by and for the West.

Whereas Jameson attributes realism's synchronicity to the "cash nexus" indicating "the synchronic role of money in the role of these individual destinies" (*Antinomies* 223), *Wizard* links it to a crisis in commodity culture as it comes to inhabit the body of the unproductive and the unemployed. In Marx, the profit of the commodity is measured in the productive time units of the working body over the time units needed to reproduce the worker—the commodity absorbs and alienates the time of the worker's life. In *Wizard*, the lifetime of the organic body appears simultaneously as machine death: body parts are replaced with European surrogate technologies and machines, with the Minister of Foreign Affairs, Machokali, flying to Europe to have his eyes surgically enlarged; the Minister of State, Sikiokuu, having his ears enlarged; and the Minister of Information, Mambo, having his lips and tongue enlarged. "I tell you," says a surgeon charged with treating a linguistic ailment, "it is not just one or two on whom I have operated and removed bits of iron buried deep in their bellies or their joints—their knees, for instance" (624). The body is here made of broken, dysfunctional, fragmented machine parts bought from the West, or deadened future time.

Though Marx theorized alienation in the context of commodity production, *Wizard* treats alienation as devoid of production and so also devoid of working or productive language. Just as in *The Eustace Diamonds,* the available classifications of property in legal language are out of sync with the type of property represented in the diamonds, Kamiti the Wizard cannot recognize the storyteller A. G.'s version of his own life story as he himself wrote it. A. G. is a former police officer who left policing because he was told to read an omen in a car accident and became a wandering storyteller who repeats the story of the Wizard before audiences in bars.[23] Aloud, Kamiti challenges the storyteller, but the storyteller does not recognize him, and the bar-goers are immersed in the storyteller's performance of Kamiti's story, thinking Kamiti is but a drunk: "He [Kamiti] felt like a writer whose work had been lifted by another only to skew its form and content" (594). As with the Ruler watching his own country on the TV news of a distant country, this detachment is no longer the "cash nexus" as much as the worker's life being taken from him by the machine of dead capital.

Antiproduction thus introduces a crisis in representation. As with work in Marx's descriptions, language loses its ability to bring worlds into existence or transform nature. This may explain *Wizard*'s frequent recurrence of language-objects that cannot be exchanged or made to signify. The chairman of the Marching to Heaven project and CEO of Eldares Modern Construction and Real Estate, Tajirika, for example—a businessman who in the end becomes defense minister and then the new ruler by having the other one killed—suffers from a rare but contagious linguistic disease where he can only say the words "If" and "If only"[24] over and over. This disease is eventually diagnosed to be caused by the stinking money bills he collects from the unemployed as bribery. Similarly, money can only exist in its concrete materiality, as an object rather than an abstract representation, signifier, or universal value against which all other objects can be compared. It is horded rather than traded; it has solid weight, is subject to gravity, and gets in the way as an encumbrance and an obstruction, like an old, out-of-place piece of machinery. Money bags shift hands, causing mishaps; money is buried in the earth; money stinks unquenchably; cash grows on trees and is harvested; an unlimited abundance of bills is meant to be dropped from a helicopter to confuse and distract the protesting crowds as well as fake fiscal largesse, but the helicopter burns and the bills were counterfeit anyway, burning and blowing away as ash.[25] If, as Marx says, money is a universal equivalent that measures and abstracts units of time spent by workers in production, here money is a technical mishap or out-of-place annoyance, inaccessible to desire or exchange, blowing away as ashes in the wind.

Piketty tells us that the growing ratio between accumulated dead capital in productive machines, on the one hand, and living labor's share (wages, reproduction) on the other is what reproduces inequality on a global level. In *Wizard*, this disproportion appears as a detachment, shown to be destructive to the worlds of living labor, a dissipation of their material worlds—finance's disinvestments in the reproductive capacities of productive workers. *Wizard* foregrounds the gothic comedy of dead labor in debt culture not as surplus or fixed capital but rather as productive obsolescence. Yet it also shows not only capital in flight but also new imaginations taking hold in its absence: the Wizard and the Voice of the People suggest a future of unleashed creativity in a dance that, like Lizzie Eustace, temporarily falls outside of power's controls. The women, defiant dancers and disruptive of the national rituals meant to commemorate foreign investments and local rule, are unidentifiable and unapprehended by the Ruler's many spies and officers of repression; the Wizard—able to change shape, form, and gender—displays, in his mirror, glimpses of images and narratives read on the fringes of reality, dreams of cracks in power's seemingly stable realities. Berardi, on the other hand, understands financial abstraction as the "'No future' culture" (51) and dead language of capitalist nihilism, "liquidating the living body of the planet and the social body of the workers' community" (52) by turning away from physical attachments ("*No Vacancy*" announces that the working body is no longer welcome here). Whereas power and property are reinstated in *The Eustace Diamonds* almost as though they were never challenged, *Wizard*'s warning is that the promise in the mirror will float up, away, and elsewhere or rot and that the dancers will surrender under repression, leaving behind empty boxes, valueless currencies, dead landscapes, and vacancies: productive potential with nowhere to go.

## *THE ROAD*

The world of dead capital in *Wizard* marks a transition from postcolonial critique. Instead of developing a rational critique of the postcolonial state, *Wizard* declares the comical emptiness of its sovereign claims in the face of even more comical financialization and debt. The state in *Wizard* is not only inefficient, perverse, corrupt, cruel, vain, and nonsensical but also a floating figure, devoid of substance and unable to belong to, represent, or act effectually inside of a particular territory, culture, nation, or population. Dead capital has become so momentous that it overpowers the representational value of democratic sovereignty, dismantling its function of redistributing some of the surplus toward producers and the reproduction of life. In fact, dead capital is so disproportional that it makes the life and needs of producers insignificant, out of sight, vaporized, and inexpressible.

Ngugi's depiction of debt's challenge to democratic governance both borrows from and surpasses a critique of the postcolonial state. Postcolonial critique is still concerned with understanding the agency available to individuals in the face of imperialist cultures to make demands on their representative states, whereas *Wizard* witnesses an incommunicability, where the state is unanswerable to local cultures because its role in motivating and reproducing laborers has been eclipsed by its role in managing the machinery of indebtedness at the expense of laborers. Marking this transition, Wole Soyinka's *The Road*, I argue, is a play still concerned with workers and their reproduction. The play is critical of the postcolonial state for its failure to deliver on the road to prosperity, and at the same time, it presents the coming-apart of old paradigms of progress through work and gives a sense of their replacement by a metaphysics of indebtedness, or sacrifice to the gods. Just as *Wizard* recognizes the distance between the Ruler and the territory he is meant to rule, *The Road* recognizes, as Phillips observes, "the gods' incompletion and loneliness without humans" (150), a loneliness to be met with a project "to build a *road* between gods and humans" (150). The invitation to communicate becomes a sacrificial debt, a terrifying obligation. Soyinka's plot of debt to development contrasts with Ngugi's version of neoliberal debt as nonprogressive time invested in building a Tower of Babel even though no such communication can be established or even imagined. I argue that the framing of Soyinka's critique of the postcolonial state points toward the beginning of a global unraveling of the conditions that make possible the reproduction of work in modernity, an unraveling that sits at the center of Ngugi's debt narrative. In today's regimes of austerity, where the role of the state in development has been challenged by policies of deregulation and public-sector dismantling demanded by global loaning institutions, worker reproduction has little interest for capital, and the commute, threatening as a horror film or absurd like a comedy, appears as the site of its collapse.

Wole Soyinka's *The Road* can be considered within a shift in the tendencies of Soyinka's oeuvre: this change becomes particularly pronounced during the Nigerian Civil War (also known as the Biafran War, 1967–70) and Soyinka's consequent incarceration,[26] but already in *The Road*, Soyinka surrenders the guarded optimism about decolonization evident in his earlier plays to a skepticism about the postcolonial moment.[27] Unlike some of his later and better-known plays, *The Road* is not a cross section of village life as it intersects directly with colonial or modern culture, foreign impositions, or systems of domination; it also does not pose an African spiritual unity against the compartmentalism demanded by Western technology and rationality, as Geoffrey Hunt alleges is characteristic of Soyinka's "nostalgia for the security of traditional values" (71) as a "response to the loss of a well-ordered universe" (70) before neocolonialism.[28] The mythological, ritualistic universe of the African gods is, in *The Road*, anything but a sweet ordering that suggests a longing for a disappearing past; rather, at the crux between local and global culture, as well as between traditionalism and modernity's accelerations, it is replete with constant mechanical accidents that cause disorder and rupture at every turn. *The Road* is an urban play that takes place at a traffic intersection where modern technology and local mythological figures quite literally dance around each other.

I argue here that *The Road* is a play about debt. It is, more or less, a rewriting of Christopher Marlowe's *The Tragical History of the Life and Death of Doctor Faustus* (c. 1592–93) through Samuel Beckett's *Waiting for Godot* (c. 1953) in the context of Africa. It thereby unites the metaphysics of Marlowe's devilish contract with Vladimir and Estragon's anticipation of death's arrival in a bleak and miserable deindustrializing landscape. It takes place in two acts, each one anticipating work to begin again while expecting an arrival that will change everything through redemption. Entering in Victorian tails and top hat, the Professor, like Lucky in *Godot* with a chair and bundles on his back, announces, like Pozzo, the dawn and the passage of time. The long-awaited visitor, the speechless mask of death (or false head in *Faustus*),[29] finally does arrive, only to create even more celebration, drumbeats, and mayhem by introducing the "power . . . [of] the knowledge of death" (228). Just as Mephistopheles collects Lucifer's debt, the Professor collects the debt to the road.[30] While *Faustus* presents Faustus's death as a repayment to the gods for his enjoyment of a life on credit—"I writ them a bill with mine own blood," admits Faustus. "The date is expired; this time is the time, and he will fetch me" (Marlowe 55)—*The Road* ends with an insistence that one owes one's life to the road: "Breathe like the road, be even like the road itself" (229), says the Professor before the mask of death, Ogun, spirals and spasms wildly, possessed, over the Professor's bleeding corpse.[31]

The plotline of owing a debt to the devil has a varied history, and of course Soyinka is not the first writer to weave it through an economic narrative and a political critique. In his conclusion to *The Consumer Society*, Jean Baudrillard treats the devil's debt as central to understanding the social alienation induced in modern commodity culture. For Baudrillard, the Faustus story imagines the subject or soul who has lost his image "hounded *to his death* by it in real life" (189). In the modern experience of alienation, the image "*takes its revenge*" (189): it "*haunts* us" (189) just as "social labour power, which, once sold, returns, through the whole social cycle of the commodity, to dispossess us of the meaning of labour itself" (190). The modern devil reflects us back to ourselves antagonistically as the social need that constantly troubles. Haunted and pursued by the image that we have sold of ourselves, we are absorbed in the signs of an impossible Affluence, the promise of progress. Written a bit earlier, Soyinka's road is strewn with the ruins of Affluence's promised construction.

I read *The Road* as constructing the preliminary contours of a "Third World" literature of global debt, of an understanding of the world in debt's terms where the reproductive end of the productive cycle has fallen outside of capital's purview and concern. Yet the criticism on Soyinka has not been particularly concerned with how his work sits at the crux of a new phase of global capitalism or how he recognizes the fallout of productive disinvestment and the failing redistributive, reproductive, and infrastructure policies of the postcolonial state.

Much of the criticism on Soyinka instead debates whether he is "authentically" African on the one hand or, on the other, echoing imperialist sensibilities. This debate dovetails with a debate about whether Soyinka's treatment of the gods is a glorification of a precolonial or premodern past to answer present problems or whether it is a projection of a more equitable future, a future of renewal. Geoffrey Hunt is most vituperative in his dismissal: "Soyinka's readership is largely a dispirited foreign bourgeoisie either seeking the exotic or displaying guilt feelings for colonialism and racism. The irony that Soyinka's readership is precisely his target of attack is merely the reflection of the greater irony that his class is dependent economically on the foreign bourgeoisie which nationalism demands that it rebels against" (74). Some of this controversy arises out of Soyinka's response to the Négritude movement initiated by Léopold Sédar Senghor in Senegal in the 1930s. Rejecting any diagnosis of African inferiority, the project of Négritude was to create a unity of African culture based in emotion and sensibility that would contrast with European reason though not be subordinated to it. Though Soyinka was at first partial to Négritude, he soon changed his mind, famously quipping, "A tiger does not proclaim his tigritude, he pounces" (as cited in Feuser 557). Yet even with his rejection of Négritude, Soyinka has himself declared that "the artist labors from an inbuilt, intuitive responsibility not only to himself, but to his roots" ("Writer" 353) and that the "artist has always functioned in African society as the recorder of mores and experience of his society *and* as the voice of vision in his own time" (356). Indeed, Soyinka was at the forefront of bringing African literatures into the curricula of African universities along with revitalizing African religions in the face of Christian and Muslim dominance. Soyinka also very clearly insists that the construction of Africanness can be wielded against power: "When ideological relations begin to deny, both theoretically and in action, the reality of a cultural entity which we define as the African world while asserting theirs even to the extent of inviting the African world to sublimate its existence in theirs, we must begin to look seriously into their political motivation" (*Myth* xi). The problem for the criticism, especially that which takes Négritude as its guidepost, might be in trying to define "Africa" singularly and essentially and so not to recognize that Soyinka is interpreting the sign "Africa" as something, temporally charged, to be struggled over.

Other critics have understood Soyinka's focus on African identity as progressive rather than regressive, oriented toward teasing out mythological elements in African cultures that may offer political alternatives. Critics such as Odun Balogun read Soyinka as turning away from the regressiveness of a nationalism based in race, as he saw in Négritude, and embracing in its stead a vision of socialism specific to the context (207). Willfried F. Feuser contests that "there is early evidence . . . of his grappling with a value system in which the main criterion is *Africanness*" (563), and he shows the closeness of Soyinka's cultural references to the cultural, artistic, linguistic, religious, and sociopolitical trajectories of the Yoruba. Whereas Hunt understands Soyinka's romanticism as a response to his "class alliance, class-ambivalence and severe cultural dislocation" (65) due to the uncertain allegiances of his compromised middle-class position, Biodun Jeyifro reads the metaphysical violence of Soyinka's plays as eruptions of "an undeclared, 'hidden' class warfare, the more bitter because it is unconscious and implosive" (13). The class conflict, he proposes, is due to a rapid urbanization devoid of an accompanying acceleration in industrialization, leading to the rise of a population left behind by development—an "'uprooted' 'reserve army of labour'" (14)—that *The Road* showcases.

Indeed, *The Road* can be said to take place in the wreckage of industrialization. Whereas *Wizard* saturates its settings in rot, pollution, and waste, the set of *The Road* is awash in the broken refuse of past production, in the "rubble of worn tyres, hubs, twisted bumpers etc." (152). In fact, not only the debris but also the drivers themselves are remainders of production's past. Though some of the critics mentioned above attribute inauthenticity to Soyinka's work in that he stages village life, pantheism, and superstition as proving the regressive character of African culture, industrialism is here what really parades as the outmoded and irrecoverable recent past. Not only the props but also the stage characters themselves are relics remaining in the dustbin of history, the refuse of progress at the crossroads of globalization. In Nigeria, "touts," explains Enoch Okpara, "can be defined as free-lance workers at railway stations, airports, ferry points, and especially motor-parks, who undertake the self-imposed responsibility of recruiting and organizing passengers who wish to travel by road, and for this work they receive a fee, or more appropriately, a 'commission', that is generally paid by the drivers of the vehicles just before their departure. All the owners are private entrepreneurs, who both compete and collaborate with one another to provide road transport for the public" (327). Okpara goes on to talk about the rise in this form of labor as resulting from a lack of investment in public transportation and a privatization, deunionization, and deregulation of such services (329). The popularity of such employment is the result of the "non-existent opportunities of employment in manufacturing" (331). *The Road* is a satire taking place on the wreckage of "Third World" industrial capitalism. Living at the usually unremarkable side of the collapsing road of development, its characters are the precursors of what will become neoliberalism's dispossessed.

Indeed, the gods serve not as a sign of cultural regression but rather as the spirit of the dying machine. *The Road* is a reenactment of an African death ritual over the corpse of Western technology. The play starts in a roadside shack, under the sign "AKSIDENT STORE—ALL PART AVAILEBUL" (151) and next to a church with a graveyard. It is six o'clock in the morning, and the touts are waking up, talking about work. There is an everydayness here, suggesting that the process of waking up for work is cyclical, daily, ceremonial, even sacred. Though the direct reference to restarting the day is clearly to the endless return to the work that awaits the drivers—"Every self-respecting tout is already in the motor park badgering passengers," says Samson, one of the touts (153)—the temporal cyclicality is also ritualized through biblical citations, elegiac proverbs, Yoruba incantations, imitations of church oratory, mystical allusions, and call-and-response rhythms. Such ritualistic language and the modern language of transport, work, and profit intertwine: "If I go chop the life so tey God so jealous me, And if he take jealousy kill me I will go start bus service between heaven and hell," says Samson, and his companion Salubi rejoins, "Sometimes na aeroplane or helicopter den go take travel for Paradise" (155). As spirit-characters of technological progress at an impasse, the gods get power in their proximity to the wreckage.

The inequality between the dead machines and the drivers is overwhelming, made visible on stage by the machine destruction mounting up in piles in the shop. In line with Piketty, the demise of industrialization is the physical sign of social polarization and inequality in *The Road*. The industrial ruins physically take over the stage. The roadside shack is the collection point for the junk left behind by those who die on the road, never getting to work. The play's action weaves between the broken and abandoned parts that had once crushed travelers: "*As his grumbling gets in stride*," read the stage directions for his defecation, "*Kotonu returns with an armful of motor parts, an old shoe, a cap etc. Goes into the mammy-waggon stall through hidden entrance upstage. He can be heard occasionally but he tries to move silently. Occasionally he lifts up the top-half tarpaulin covering and pushes out an object*" (165). Kotonu shits out broken technologies, as though his body is made of parts. The question for the drivers is not *if* they will be killed but what kind of machine will run them down and sell their parts: "If you gonna be killed by a car, you don't wanna be killed by a Volkswagen. You wanra Limousine, a Ponriac or something like that" (172). The gods' celebratory dance of death, their profiting from offerings and sacrifice, depends on modernity's technological mishaps. Productive machines—like the gods—demand the life of the worker in exchange for the promise of an affluent future in the gods' benevolence.

*The Road* thus recognizes, within the symbolic context of African religion, a population that is coming to be at the ultimate end of a beleaguered modernity. It *spiritualizes* the afterlife of a set of working conditions connected to the manufacturing class; it spiritualizes debt. While the death dirge mounts over the ruins of a prior industrial age, the touts are the dead space of industrial labor. "How can anyone buy a uniform when he hasn't got a job?" asks Samson, and Salubi responds, "Go mind your own business you jobless tout" (152). Work licenses are negotiated as debt, even when forged. "Do you think not enough people die here that you must come and threaten me with death?" Professor asks Salubi, who beseeches him for a license. "You spurious spew. You instrument of mortgage. You unlicensed appendage of the steering wheel" (184). The touts go into debt to the Professor to pay for the right to work: "So the dead are now your bank managers?" (182) asks Professor when he learns that Samson has promised to pay the fees for his counterfeit license from the money buried in the churchyard.

Not only does the Professor control the issuance of work permits, albeit forged ones. Also, the Professor enters the stage bearing the road sign "BEND," with which he can alter the physical territory, the terrain of production and reproduction. By plucking the word out of the earth, the Professor can change what travelers see when they come around the curve, causing them to lose their way or change course, just as the erection of the Tower of Babel changes the terrain of Paradise in *Wizard*. "I have a new wonder to show you," boasts the Professor, "a madness where a motor-car throws itself against a tree—Gbram! And showers of crystal flying on broken souls . . . They died, all three of them, crucified on rigid branches" (158). Here, the sign has the power to induce the sacrifice to the gods by causing the mechanical failures and also by simultaneously changing the touts' certain knowledge of the objective world where workers lives are reproduced. The sacrificial bodies of former commuters are turned into corrupted, nonproductive machines and dead communication, or dead labor for exchange. Progress morbidly sucks out their lives.

*The Road* expresses an awareness that national production is unable to fuel the forward movement of progress: indebted to the future through progress, the postcolonial state came upon a curve on the road to progress and crashed, surrendering its remains to thieves and thugs. Instead of taking up solely a political critique or allegory, *The Road* submits that the power of antiproduction is mythological—that is, unidentifiable within human scale, unreachable, overwhelming, sublime. The sacredness of the word demands a permanent dispossession. By removing the sign, the Professor also usurps the drivers' ability to confer meaning on the future through participating in the building up of the social and semiotic world in production.

*The Road* previews what will become a culture devoted to debt, where the road to production has come to an end, buried in its own wreckage. It provides a critique of the postcolonial state that is prescient—in fact, a critique of the postcolonial state that offers an intimation that it is nudging toward the throes of neoliberal antiproduction. The sign "BEND" abolishes reality by opposing the material world. The material world, in fact, has become irrelevant to the sign's circulation, unequal to it, *something else.*[32] As Berardi elaborates, "Capitalism is no longer able to semiotize and to organize the social potency of cognitive productivity, because value can no longer be defined in terms of the average necessary time of labor, and therefore the old forms of private property and salary are no longer able to semiotize and organize the deterritorialized existence of capital and social labor" (74). *The Road* interprets the new life of the sign as metaphysical, conferred by the call of the dead, telling a story of play, pleasure, and jest in the nonconforming merriment of the African gods. *Wizard of the Crow*, meanwhile, critiques the distancing of semiotic and productive power and accumulation as political. The gods have been replaced by the distant bankers, financiers, and power elite who strip the unemployed of their infrastructure the way the Professor commands that the drivers strip the dead for his profit.

## CONCLUSION

Zygmunt Bauman locates a new type of human waste in refugee and immigrant camps in Europe and racialized inner-city ghettos in the United States, the "dumping ground [for those for whom] the surrounding society has no economic or political use" (81) and are abandoned to "the nowhere-land of non-humanity" (80). The unemployed here are, as Bauman says, warnings about the unraveling of the institutional power through which citizens in a democracy have historically demanded redress and recognition. They are the present manifestations of a future exposed to economic globalization but devoid of political globalization, an eventuality where multinational financial power can force us, without protections, to sell future savings and accumulation to pay for others' present enrichment and empowerment. Like the indebted, Bauman's immigrants, because they are stateless, are outside of the scope of effective institutional action, as state institutions are beyond the reach of their demands and outside of the touch of their suffering.

In fact, neoliberal debt ensures that the state is unreactive to citizens' demands because it requires the state to sell off its means of command, its means of redistributing national income as well as its means of building productivities—its infrastructure—to distant and disinterested investors and stakeholders. The indebted compel an awareness of the sinister outcome of infrastructural collapse. As Ivan Ascher inquires, "What should we make of the fact that even our *promises* are now being made only to be 'sold' or otherwise exchanged, as if the mere buying and selling of financial assets were sufficient to turn an uncertain future into a source of security in the present?" (14). For Ascher as for Ngugi, debt *is in the process of replacing the commodity*. Because it is replacing the commodity, debt is also replacing and even destroying the commodity's apparatus: the mechanisms of social reproduction at the state, technical, ideological, and institutional levels. Therefore, the kinds of infrastructural divestment that Bauman identifies as leading to mass population upheavals, immigrant crises, and zones of precarious, volatile, and unregulated employment (when employment exists) have become sources of profit: places where destructive liens on the infrastructure can be cut up and recombined to be sold as securities and bonds, as in Puerto Rico.

In the wake of the 2017 hurricanes Irma and Maria, which hit Puerto Rico directly, the status of Puerto Rico and its debt is up in the air. Both the federal and local governments have had ineffectual responses because the island has run out of money to pay for repairs and reconstruction after the massive devastation, particularly to its energy infrastructure. Six weeks after the hurricane hit, a large majority of the island still lacked electricity; roads were impassible; and the island's schools reopened with only 9 percent of the students returning. As a result, Puerto Rico was turned into a police state. Four months later, more than half of Puerto Ricans were still without electricity, celebrating Christmas in the dark, and estimations were that energy would not be completely restored for another five months (another power outage occurred in April 2018 due to a downed transmission line, causing a total blackout and putting recovery efforts behind once again). Eleven months after the storm, in August 2018, energy company PREPA finally announced that all its power grids were restored, even as critics have noted they are still vulnerable to future storms, which are likely. After Irma and Maria, 167 schools were closed, while nine months later, plans were put in place to close 265 more. The Jones Act was temporarily suspended for ten days and then reinstated, while trucks were not able to distribute goods because of inoperable roads. A quarter of a million people lost their homes. Even though the government reported officially only sixty-four deaths (allowing President Trump to boast about how his own administration's recovery efforts excelled over the Obama administration's), Arelis R. Hernández and Laurie McGinley reported in the *Washington Post* that 4,645 died as a result of Hurricane Maria (within a small margin of error). According to a study done by

Harvard University and the Beth Israel Deaconess Medical Center (Kishore et al.) to which they refer, 14.3 deaths occurred for every 1,000 residents through December 31, 2017 (70 percent above the official number; after that time, the data became unavailable to the researchers), with $90 billion in damages (the second costliest storm in US history). The deaths were attributed to lack of access to medical services, slow recovery, telecommunications failures, lack of water and essential services, unsafe and unhealthy conditions, and an incapacitated power grid. Many left the island.

The federal response and recovery efforts did not considerably improve Puerto Rico's ability to maintain the distribution of basic needs: water, energy, food, transportation, housing, health care, education, and medications. At first, PREPA signed a $300 million contract with a small Montana firm, Whitefish Energy, that had only two employees. Whitefish was the only company bidding for the contract that did not demand payment upfront, as other companies presumably would not trust Puerto Rico's ability to meet the increase in debt obligation. The contract had to be canceled by the governor of Puerto Rico, Ricardo Rosselló, because of corruption in the contract bidding (but the canceled contract still had to be paid for, as FEMA [the Federal Emergency Management Agency] refused to cover the costs).[33] The CEO of PREPA, Ricardo Ramos, canceled numerous congressional appearances. FEMA denied responsibility even though the contract explicitly says that FEMA is responsible.[34] An emergency manager appointed by PROMESA's board to oversee any further contracts then resigned on November 10. Even after the Army Corps of Engineers and other contractors reached the island, supplies and equipment for the repairs were slow in arriving, with fifty thousand power poles still needing to be replaced four months in. One year after the storm, a warehouse was found stacked with bottled water, which never made it to the storm's victims.

In January 2018, armed federal agents from FEMA and the US Army Corps of Engineers stormed a PREPA warehouse to retrieve equipment essential for Puerto Rican recovery and the restoration of power. Kate Aronoff of *The Intercept* reported that the workers brought in from the mainland were finding it virtually impossible to do the necessary work because of the lack of equipment. Aronoff attributed PREPA's mismanagement to deregulation, which, under the guise of cost savings, was actually causing the reduction of tax revenues by encouraging Puerto Ricans to leave the island, fed up with the outage. Though the Puerto Rico Energy Commission had started to pass some reforms between 2013 and 2016—including some that moved the island toward renewable energy, allowed for the development of microgrids at the local level, controlled rates with an eye to affordability, and established the Independent Office for Consumer Protection—the new governor appointments under the Fiscal Oversight Board believe that structural adjustment is necessary for Puerto Rico to solve "the crisis" and propose consolidation of five of the regulatory agencies (including energy) to keep down public expenses, even though the Energy Commission had been totally funded by ratepayers (Aronoff, "Armed Federal Agents"). This move will result in the rollback of the Energy Commission's regulatory framework.

The press coverage is divided on the status of the debt in the wake of the hurricane and recovery. The owners of the debt are growing worried, as the government will soon be out of money. Noting that none of Puerto Rico's creditors offered anything but thoughts and prayers to assist in recovery, Aronoff raises the possibility that the PROMESA board could block collection on the debt obligations, either by repackaging the remaining debt and holding onto it until the economy gets back on track or through a federal bailout. On the flip side, the creditors could manage to overturn PROMESA's board and the bankruptcy process, giving creditors the go-ahead to extract repayments before Puerto Rico's infrastructure and production have been restored (Aronoff, "Puerto Rico").

Yet as Elizabeth Yeampierre and Naomi Klein also point out in *The Intercept*, hurricane aid, given to Florida and Texas in the form of grants, was given to Puerto Rico as a House-approved relief package in the form of $5 billion in loans. Though $81 billion was pledged by Congress for hurricane recovery relief, that amount was shared with affected zones in Texas and Florida as well as with areas in California hit by wildfires. The governor of Puerto Rico said that $90 billion were needed for Puerto Rico alone. Meanwhile, President Trump's signature tax bill will deepen Puerto Rico's burden by increasing taxes on goods manufactured on the island and going to the US mainland, even as businesses are leaving due to the difficulties of operating without electricity, reducing treasury collections further. The federal government is initiating policies that will thrust Puerto Rico deeper into debt while still angering the creditors. Puerto Ricans are left in the care of a weakened managerial control board with fewer resources to fend off the debt collectors.[35] It is highly likely that Puerto Rico's infrastructure will be mortgaged further.

The case of Puerto Rico demonstrates that the metaphor of progress that Soyinka invokes through the road is no longer operable. The idea of even semiemployed, temporary contractors who can turn the refused surplus or waste of old production into amassed capital for producing augmented future profit is defunct. Soyinka foresaw the morbid degradation of industrial infrastructure in Nigeria and the dance of death that ensued, but he saw this as a continuous process reproducing inequality as a constant, caused by postcolonial corruption: the workday was still an endless repetition, returning like a ritual. Soyinka treated debt as a metaphysics, a compromise that linked the local gods with technological progress, rather than as the death of production altogether, the emancipation of value from the things that sustained it, and the worldly destruction that follows. Soyinka did not foresee what Ngugi observed: that the pathway to progress was mortgaged out as a false promise before it ever came to be. Ngugi understands debt as a governing force that imposes inequality, unemployment, and unproductivity as a mechanism of financial extraction at the origin point of "Third World" identities.

The shift in thinking about debt in the "Third World" from Soyinka to Ngugi supplements a divide in their thinking about literary representation. In the previous chapter, I showed how Trollope used Lizzie's diamonds as an object lesson in finance: the diamond necklace was an object that, despite its anticipated solidity as rock, did not consistently remain solid or substantial and could not be identified in relation to an extension of a particular space, law, or placement. As such, the existing categories of value, property, and ownership could not apply to the necklace, despite attempts by lawyers, nobility, jewelers, robbers, and various stakeholders to clarify their essential character. The meaning of the diamonds within the financial system that they were supposed to bring into view and comprehension was dependent on the diamonds also appearing within literary realism as a failure of the real, a symbol that at once has a concrete presence but, in its circulation, could not hold that presence intact.

Soyinka and Ngugi differ in their response to the challenge of the literary symbol as it substantiates social relations inside of systems of finance in the twenty-first-century "Third World." Soyinka, like Trollope, sees the sign taken away from the ground that it created, confusing those with expectations of its once-credible certainty. When it is taken away, those without the sign experience its absence as a confusion and a travesty. The absence causes mass fatalities because it reintroduces uncertainty, and the uncertainty encourages negotiations and sacrifices to the gods in a search for certainty. The play suggests that the balance that the sign upheld has been troubled; without it, the road is made unpassable and even unreal. For Ngugi, on the other hand, language is the first casualty of debt. In fact, debt exposes that language never secured what it referenced but also that language never belonged in the first place—that its referentiality was a trick, a false promise of security in things in living time, a destructive impulse sold under a sunny but cynical slogan of plenty. With debt divorcing capital from the territory of the living, just as when value is emancipated from referring to things, words also no longer touch on living flesh, and value is created without investments in working bodies. Unlike in Soyinka, where the sign circulates, is stolen, and is struggled over (like the diamonds) on a road in perpetual decline, in *Wizard of the Crow*, the financial system devastates the exchange of signs before its Tower is even built. As debt forces disinvestments from areas of production, *Wizard* reminds us, it destroys the correspondence between language and reality through an "annihilation of reality," with both production and reproduction brought to a standstill.

Ironically, perhaps, the destruction of the material world that *Wizard* envisions corresponds with a return of the supernatural, now in the hands of political opposition to power and domination. The Wizard can heal the catastrophe of postcolonial modernity by holding up a mirror and thus restoring living time, giving back life to the world of real people flashing up behind the fake image of Paradise basking in the financial largess of the Global Bank. "Here, in the new venture," *Wizard* concludes, "the extraordinary, the magical, the wonderful, and even the strange came out of the ordinary and the familiar . . . Knowledge is the discovery of the magic of the ordinary. Like words put into song" (758–59). Lodged here in a romantic fantasy with the flare of magical realism, the everyday world of material practices, both productive and reproductive, as Ngugi recognizes them, is vanishing behind a veneer of power and can only be accessed as a magical desire appearing in fragments of reflective glass. The mirror suggests glimpses, moments that have escaped from debt's capture of time where the future has been sold elsewhere, but these moments exist in evanescent and ephemeral reflections only. As Simon Morgan Wortham specifies, "Debt itself aggresses against temporal continuity in general. If this is true, then debt's supposed commitment to the unstinting continuity and continuation of the present for all future time to come (as an unbreakable expression of power) itself becomes questionable and resistible, not just as an idea but in terms of the practical possibilities suggested by the limit or deficit between what debt *wants* and what it *is*." Here, supposedly, resistance can be worked into the break between debt's golden promises for the future and debt's present exploitative practices.

The strategy of suggesting possibilities and pointing out limits or of revealing that everyday practices of production and reproduction still exist as fantastical projections in magical mirrors seems unsatisfactory, or maybe just a beginning. Within the current organization of economic, political, and military power, resisting debt by pointing out its contradictions—even in the form of refusing payment or defaulting—will be punitive. The reality is that debt itself is the fantasy; it is a struggle over the means of representing what counts as value. Since the financial system required a reorientation in economic thinking, where belief in representational values substituted for assuming the intrinsic value in things—finance's "dereferentialization"—much of what counts as financial value is manipulations of the imaginary, representations of credibility, and the symbolic production of trust. In practice, debt attributes obligations to producers who have to borrow back the profits they have made for others. Debt's systems blame inequality on unequal people rather than understanding inequality as intrinsic to capital's representations of itself and its histories of exploitation, as antagonistic and irreconcilable. Extending political globalization in parallel to economic globalization would mean not assuming that some are unequal by nature of their identities or their geographies and then faulting them financially, setting them up as originally disadvantaged in order to prove that they cannot meet the standards of democratic citizenship and productive vitality and, as such, extracting surplus by charging them still more. Extending political globalization would perhaps allow broader participation in deciding how the goods of the earth might be more equitably and justly shared. Debt needs not only an emancipation of its temporalities but also, more fundamentally, a reorientation of the semiotics of value toward territory, responsibility, and global citizenship—a reorientation that should lead, ultimately, to debt's cancellation.

# Notes

## INTRODUCTION

1. As social and political scientist Geoffrey Ingham explains it, "By the late twentieth century, it has become clear to the monetary authorities of all major capitalist economies that central banks have very little choice, *in the short term*, but to supply funds to enable the commercial banks to balance their books and to augment their reserves after they have met the demand for loans. Apart from any other considerations, not to accede to these requests would jeopardize the liquidity of the payments system" (137). What he is saying is that the banks essentially took over the monetary system of money creation. I find his emphasis on "the short term" to be puzzling. The evidence he uses for the necessity of the transfer of monetary policy to the banks is a justificatory quote from the Bank of England.
2. Geoffrey Ingham also wants to establish that creditworthiness, and thus the supply of credit (or money), is socially constructed. What he understands as creditworthiness, however, is the social conditions of what makes a person creditworthy: "Loans by the banking system are priced in accordance with a profit-making strategy that includes a calculation of the degree of risk of default. First, risk is taken to increase with the length of the term of the loan; second, it is considered to vary with the purpose of the loan . . . ; and third, the borrowers' ability to repay—creditworthiness—is assessed" (137). From what we saw in 2008, this type of assessment, if it is meant to have an empirical reference, seems but an academic pipe dream. He goes on to say, "Apart from the higher levels of capitalist finance, credit rating is now a formal and almost completely depersonalized procedure, based on computer database information" (137).

3. Ironically, J. P. Morgan was surprised at the surge of collateralized debt obligations (CDOs). As John Lanchester goes on to tell, though they invented the instrument, they could not envision it without in-depth research into the business: "They could see how profitable the new-mortgage-backed versions of their CDOs were. But after taking a long, hard look at the new business, they took a pass. They simply didn't see how the risks were being engineered down to a safe level . . . Blythe Masters, the woman in charge of the *Exxon Valdez* deal . . . , and thus one of the creators of the entire CDS [credit default swap] industry, was baffled by the CDO boom. 'How are the other banks doing it?' she asked. 'How are they making so much money?' According to Gillian Tett in *Fool's Gold*, 'she was so steeped in the ways of J. P. Morgan that it never occurred to her that the other banks might simply ignore all the risk controls J. P. Morgan had adhered to'" (121). Lanchester is using this example to argue against the bankers who claimed that they had to use these methods to be competitive. J. P. Morgan, according to Andrew Ross Sorkin of the *New York Times*, is currently, however, projecting large losses in the face of the new tax bill. Sorkin suggests that the fall in profits has to do with new regulations in fixed-income trading, what he calls a "keystone product," which had declined about a quarter of its income in the past five years. This would seem to imply, contra Sorkin's own assessment, that Wall Street's huge profits were contingent on J. P. Morgan's practices being made unprofitable and obsolete.
4. Thanks are due to Robin D. G. Kelley for recommending this text to me.
5. This goes against any goal of global well-being or even efficiency. As Samir Amin (among many others) notes, "History shows that the gains brought about by increases in productivity are greatly superior to those that can be obtained through competitive advantage in the best of cases. History also shows that relative prices are not determined by the market, but by the social conditions, beyond supply and demand, in which production operates" (27).

## CHAPTER 1

1. "The Puerto Rico Electric Power Authority" was founded in 1941 with the mission "to provide electric energy services to our customers in the most efficient, cost-effective and reliable manner in harmony with the environment." PREPA advertises itself as "one of the major public electric power corporations in the United States" and is directed by a government board that has seven members appointed by the governor of Puerto Rico and two members elected by the company's clients. See http://www.prepa.com/aeees_eng.asp.

2. *The Eustace Diamonds* has recently attracted the attention of "thing theory." Stephanie Markovits, for example, discusses it in relation to neoformalism, as together they challenge genre. Describing Trollope's diamonds as "sliding uncannily between literal and figurative manifestations" (608), Markovits, however, does not link this finding to finance or even to commodification. *The Eustace Diamonds* comes from a time, as Jonathan Plotz depicts it, when portable property was beginning to merge the sentimental values of the subject with the impersonal value of objects in the marketplace that the eighteenth century had separated out, where there would be no choice between "the world of true value and the world of fluid exchange" (337). Though this insight is certainly valuable for thinking of the transition toward a commodity-based economy, it does not explain the times when the diamonds are both physically present and absent at the same time or represented as present even without physical presence, a tendency that hints toward the rise of a financialized or speculative economy that the diamonds are meant, in my argument, to help figure out.
3. John Lanchester wrote *I.O.U.* while doing research for his 2013 *Capital: A Novel*. This novel is very aware of its nineteenth-century antecedents. It takes place in a London city street that is the contemporary version of a Trollopian village. Instead of mingling in and about aristocratic properties, the plot takes place as the global middle-class inhabitants of the houses on that street interact, whether or not their lifelines and social activities cross paths. The year 2008 ushers in a fall in the value of the houses that affects these modes of interaction; like the diamonds, the houses carry the effects of financial crisis.
4. As Patrick Brantlinger has indicated, in the nineteenth century, "there is a symbiosis between money and novelistic realism that seems especially significant in making it also the era of high nationalism and imperialism" (143). John Reed reads the mid-nineteenth century as a time when money took a new guise in literature, on the one hand, because of the 1866 crash and 1873 panic, where the economy did not recover as expected so there was a loss of confidence, and, on the other, because of an enlarged middle class, where "more people sought to acquire their share of the nation's wealth" (181).
5. "The Puerto Rico Oversight, Management, and Economic Stability Act" establishes an oversight board and provides for debt restructuring and infrastructure projects.
6. Kathy Alexis Posmiades reads *The Eustace Diamonds* as marking a moment when "heirloom culture," or inalienability and inheritance, is being replaced by the culture of the contract, or commodification. The idea that diamonds are heirlooms, passed down through the generations along the male line,

or the idea that women are traded to create alliances between their patriarchal families, harkens back to a time before commodification, and Trollope's novel shows the new looking back on a culture that no longer makes sense: "Trollope's novel thus goes out of its way to create a world in which actual economic relations and activities run counter to metaphorical economic relations and activities" (98).

7. As Jeff Nunokawa writes, "If capital assumes the forms of the novel, so does the property that eludes it . . . When property is released from the mortal coils of capital in the fiction I will scrutinize here, it does so *as* fiction, as a rhetorical afterlife that arises from the ashes of exchange, as a fragment of literary fantasy . . . , and as a narrative whose always anticipated conclusion never comes" (14). Elsie Michie also remarks, "Wealth, after midcentury, ceased to be defined as a substance and instead began to be regarded as an intangible force" (108). Both these critics understand Trollope's novels as working out this transition. Mary Poovey identifies political economists in the eighteenth-century writing on this issue: "Tories like Lord Bolingbroke and Edmund Burke insisted that all credit money was pernicious because it undermined the hegemony of property, which was the true, because natural, ground of value" (*Genres* 64). By the mid-nineteenth century, she says, political economists were referring back to what was a controversy in the eighteenth century as outside of debate, only acknowledging the pro-money side, because the issue of money had become settled, more or less.
8. For example, "Why," asks John Sutherland in the introduction to the Penguin edition, "is Lizzie Eustace so consistently and embarrassingly in debt?" (24).
9. The analogy to the word *citizen* in the first part of the chapter should be clear. *Citizen* is an abstraction, a fiction to which rights are attached. Its reference ought to be general, meaning certain formal properties that would potentially apply to anyone within the given territory. Yet because the application to particular (racial) threatened qualities of the formal generality of citizenship, manipulations had to be made to impose moral badness on certain of its referents—in this case by establishing race as a moral category in contrast to citizenship, making them nonreferents and therefore rightsless.
10. As Lady Glencora—the wife of the future prime minister—laments to Lizzy, "All is not gold that glistens, Lady Eustace" (Trollope, *Eustace* 535).
11. Andrew Miller writes, "The most remarkable thing about the titular diamonds themselves is how rarely we see them" (160). Miller understands *The Eustace Diamonds* as communicating within a transition to possessive commodity culture, where, nevertheless, "the representation of material culture . . . is extraordinarily thin" (160).

12. This question of the economy's relation to substance—questions unleashed by the diamonds—surfaces still in debates about the current economic crises. Joshua Clover, for example, analyzes the value theory of labor as understanding a clear production basis for the economy, where the limits to growth can be found in the actual limits of the laborer's life and exertion, as opposed to *autonomista* perspectives, where production has been taken over by pure circulation, and the real economy has been superseded. This "changed character" (Clover, "Value/Theory/Crisis" 110) of capitalism would warrant a capitalism without physical referents, which would coincide historically with the "linguistic turn" of the humanities in the 1970s and beyond. Clover sees this as an error in Marxism, as early as Marx's own writings, which insisted that profits had to be made from labor (surplus value) and could not be made in the disparity of value and price in commodity circulation: "The rise in finance is correlated with the rise of both speculative value and immaterial labor—but this indicates a problem in production, not a new source or mode. Finance is neither cause nor solution for this problem but its veil" (ibid., 112). Including the disparity of price and value in the analysis would mean, for Clover, that the immateriality of production that interested the *autonomistas* like Antonio Negri and Christian Marazzi was always part of accumulation through production and not evidence of a historical transformation.
13. According to Poovey, "Today's general reader, who likes these novels because they are 'realistic' (true to life), keeps alive the informational function (they remind us of how things used to be), whose renunciation enabled nineteenth-century writers to elevate the genre" (*Genres* 356). Given a novelist like Trollope, it is difficult to agree that he had renounced completely the informational aspect of imaginative writing, considering the material aspects of writing, such as bills, checks, letters, and legal opinions, that frequently surface in the work. Rather, Trollope in *The Eustace Diamonds* reveals the connections between conveying information and the narrative conventions of the novel.
14. "If, however, only the particular is given, for which the universal is to be found, then the power of judgment is merely reflecting" (Kant 67). Another term of Kant's that might be useful here is *imagination*: "The powers of cognition that are set into play by this representation are hereby in a free play, since no determinate concept restricts them to a particular rule of cognition" (102). The difference is that "reflecting judgment" is linked to an experience of nature as nature herself gives order, whereas the "imagination" is linked to representations inside intuition.
15. According to Stephen Ross, it is modernism's interest in aestheticism and spiritualism that gives it, in distinction to prior tendencies, "the incitement

to speculate as the locus of value" (143), and speculation—the expansion of money value across material borders by means of the imaginary—allows the experience of the future, the ethical, and the unknown to be read inside the present.

16. "Every credit economy is also an economy of debt, and, during these centuries in particular, English investors' extraordinary rate of return on their capital was largely obtained through overseas investment. As a consequence, to omit all discussion of India and the West Indies, in particular, is to present an admittedly one-sided picture of the global system of credit and debt whose legacy still casts such a long shadow across the world" (Poovey, *Genres* 23).
17. Bowen, without citing particular texts, describes "the central importance of written communication to the domestic management of the Company's overseas affairs" (151), including literature (153), as part of the excessive communicational bureaucracy developed to govern the company's affairs intercontinentally and earn the consensus of the British public.
18. "*This oscillation is at once a law of movement and the possibility of crisis*. This oscillation is the form of existence of value, the continuous commutation and the essential duality of value [between use and exchange]. This oscillation is the revelation of the social relation which in reality extends itself, the mode in which is consolidated exchangeability as an exclusive social relation [exchangeability wins as abstraction and alienation]. This oscillation is thus, still and always, the possibility of crisis" (Negri 29; original emphasis). For Negri, use value never settles down and surrenders.
19. "In the realm of fiction, the negative connotations associated with invalid money were neutralized by the claim that imaginative writing did not have to refer to anything in the actual world . . . Fiction, which was not held to a standard of referential accuracy, [helped] readers practice trust, tolerate deferral, evaluate character, and, in a general sense, believe in things that were immaterial" (Poovey, *Genres* 89).
20. The overlapping of the thinking on currency and credit with a hatred of aesthetics can be seen in a comparison of the first pages of some of Trollope's other major novels chronologically on either side of *The Eustace Diamonds*. *The Last Chronicle of Barset*, for example—Trollope's 1867 finale to his Barsetshire series—is the story of a county priest, Mr. Crawley, who accidentally uses a check that is not his to pay a debt to the local butcher. "I can never bring myself to believe it" (7), begins the novel. What the attorney's daughter could not believe was that Mr. Crawley purposely paid a bill with somebody else's check, claiming that the check had been signed to him, a statement that turned out to be false. Meanwhile, *The Way We Live Now*, Trollope's 1875 satire

about financial failure, begins with Lady Carbury, thought by critics to be a "female literary charlatan" (12), trying to use her beauty as a woman to win good reviews from a respected newspaper editor and a literary journal for her less-than-valuable work of "Literature" that Trollope sarcastically crowns with a capital *L*. In both instances, instead of measuring the real value contained in real things, financial value is derided in terms of its affiliations with the uncertainties introduced by the aesthetics of writing in a market society.

21. "Between the 1850s and the 1860s, the charge of fictitiousness lost its force, and attention turned to the subjective experience of financial groundedness. I have been arguing that this shift, from probing financial logics to pursuing psychological perspectives, comprises a problematic psychologism: systematic analysis of the 'case of metaphysics' was displaced by impressionistic exploration of affect. Where fictitious capital made the financial economy inexplicably complex, defiantly elusive of exposition, the psychic economy realized capital, domesticating the economy as the natural issue of interiority . . . Psychology lent a ground to economic relations" (Kornbluh, *Realizing Capital* 39–43). Ericka Beckman also notices the intersections among financial representations, psychological imbalance, and character construction in nineteenth- and early twentieth-century fiction, but in Latin America "the realist novel ultimately rests on foundations of credit and belief that are . . . shaky and illusory," highlighting "finance capital as an illusory and indeed fictive form of wealth" (97). For Beckman, the unstable psychologies of such realist characters reflect "the invisible and abstract forces through which [national] wealth is generated and destroyed" (92). "I am interested," she notes, "in exploring the striking similarities between . . . [the] imbalanced psyche and the imbalance of peripheral economy, which instead of reaching balance or surplus, runs in the other direction, toward crisis and bankruptcy" (132–33).
22. Until 1867, when diamonds were discovered in South Africa and other colonies, all diamonds—including, most prominently, Queen Victoria's own—came from India and involved exploitative extraction. The discovery of more mines meant that the precious jewels might find themselves in hands other than royal ones.
23. As Jeff Nunokawa writes, "If capital assumes the forms of the novel, so does the property that eludes it . . . When property is released from the mortal coils of capital in the fiction I will scrutinize here, it does so *as* fiction, as a rhetorical afterlife that arises from the ashes of exchange, as a fragment of literary fantasy . . . , and as a narrative whose always anticipated conclusion never comes" (14).

24. For example, "Events like the collapse of the South Sea Bubble not only exposed the existence of the fact/fiction continuum in a monetary instrument; they also fueled public intolerance for this continuum" (*Genres* 83).
25. Poovey elucidates, "The breakup of the fact/fiction continuum was modeled on the distinction between valid and invalid monetary tokens; this distinction, in turn, was the necessary precondition for making representative money seem to *be* rather than simply to *represent* value" (*Genres* 61). The abundance of cases of counterfeit and fraud point to the insufficiencies in this economy of trust.
26. An 1876 article in *Blackwood's Edinburgh Magazine* tells of a joint-stock company that exists as a personage. The document travels in the pockets of various men of business. The "sham prospectus" (Oliphant 98) was originally written and promoted by a crafty army officer who was also a member of Parliament, whose job it was to build a story that would, in time, make something that is nothing seem as something of value. The company, duping the public, eventually succumbs to its own swindle.
27. "My long career upon town—" the counterfeit coin confesses, "in the course of which I have been bitten, and run, and subjected to the most humiliating tests—has blunted my sensibilities, while it has taken off the sharpness of my edges; and, like the counterfeits of humanity, whose lead may be seen emulating silver at every turn, my only desire is—not to be worthy of passing, but simply—to pass" (Blanchard 421).
28. "If literature is a particular form by means of which objective reality is reflected, then it becomes of crucial importance for it to grasp that reality as it truly is, and not merely to confine itself to reproducing whatever manifests itself immediately and on the surface. If a writer strives to represent reality as it truly is, i.e. if he is an authentic realist, then the question of totality plays a decisive role, no matter how the writer actually conceives the problem intellectually . . . The literary practice of every true realist demonstrates the importance of the overall objective social context, and the 'insistence on all-round knowledge' required to do it justice" (1037). Lukacs is citing Lenin here.
29. I am reliant here on Deidre Shauna Lynch's descriptions of narratives of talking money in the late eighteenth century / early nineteenth century in *The Economy of Character: Novels, Market Culture, and the Business of Inner Meaning*. Lynch is interested in the facelessness of the eighteenth-century "gentleman" who is sympathetic to all experience that he encounters, as it gives way in the nineteenth century to the particularity of character: "The coin's or banknote's adventures closely resemble those of the gentleman who knows what it is to enter into sociable exchanges with all and sundry. (Conversely, it is the possession of

these coins and banknotes that expedites the gentleman's exemplary mobility.) Money is, after all, an appropriate vehicle for a narrative form organized to enable readers to collect the characters of experience by collecting characters in the other sense of the term" (96). The circulation of money reflects the career of the "gentleman" as an abstraction that can be universally exchanged; the counterfeit coin is similarly abstract but also exhibits particularities.

30. The six Palliser novels compose Trollope's second series after his famous series, the Chronicles of Barsetshire (1855–67). They span from *Can You Forgive Her?* in 1864 to *The Duke's Children* in 1879. Whereas the Barsetshire novels deal with politics among the clergy in villages, the Palliser novels focus on parliamentary politics, mostly in London but also in the country homes of the elite. *The Eustace Diamonds* is the third in the Palliser series.
31. Parliament would decide "as to whether the Sawab of Mygawb should have twenty millions of rupees paid to him and be placed upon the throne, or whether he should be kept in prison all his life" (Trollope, *Eustace* 63).
32. Goodlad reads the ritual displays of power as expressing Trollope's idea that the British Empire would grow through the spread of these Barsetshire-type "heirlooms" (7) (replicating the forms of British class power in India), though he did not think India suitable.
33. Lizzie's debt is similar to what Richard Sennett describes as "the 'mystification' of material life in public, especially in the matter of clothes, caused by mass production and distribution" (19), where, within the urban chaos of nineteenth-century social life, "public markings were losing distinctive forms" (20). Though everyone could appear the same and equal, says Sennett, nobody really believed that people were the same, and so the presence of strangers dressed up in familiar attire was unsettling to the codes by which people recognized each other.

## CHAPTER 2

1. Shohat uses the term *Third World* as clearing the space for active critique: "Coined in the fifties in France by analogy to the third estate (the commoners, all those who were neither the nobility nor the clergy), the term 'Third World' gained international currency in both academic and political contexts, particularly in reference to anticolonial nationalist movements of the fifties through the seventies as well as to the political-economic analysis of dependency theory and world system theory" (100).
2. Simon Gikandi calls this an "unnamed African country" in the first part of his review (158) but later does return to the name (159). The ambiguity is

unexplained. Since names of things and people are often changing in *Wizard of the Crow*, one wonders if this discrepancy is a mistake or part of the point of Gikandi's critique.

3. "The death instinct," remark Deleuze and Guattari, "that is its name, and death is not without a model. For desire desires death also, because the full body of death is its motor, just as it desires life . . . Desiring-machines work only when they break down, and by continually breaking down" (8).
4. For Beckman, Latin American novels register a distrust in financial investments as a road to development or prosperity, given the instabilities caused by swindles, fraud, and massive withdrawals of European speculation and the ensuing crises. "Imbalance and anomaly," she observes, "express the contradictions of peripheral capitalist development" (132) in Latin American novels of financialization, revealing economic instabilities as endemic for peripheral economies by linking them to mental instabilities and debilitating nervous crises. This description resonates for *Wizard*.
5. Bakhtin writes, "But the centripetal forces of the life of language, embodied in 'unitary language,' operate in the midst of heteroglossia. At any given moment of its evolution, language is stratified not only into linguistic dialects in the strict sense of the word (according to formal linguistic markers, especially phonetic) but also—and for us this is the essential point—into languages that are socio-ideological: languages of social groups . . . Alongside the centripetal forces, the centrifugal forces of language carry on their uninterrupted work; alongside verbal-ideological centralization and unification, the uninterrupted processes of decentralization and disunification go forward. Every concrete utterance of a speaking subject serves as a point where centrifugal as well as centripetal forces are brought to bear" (271–72).
6. In response to Nietzsche's *Genealogy of Morals*, Deleuze and Guattari write, "It is not because everyone is suspected, in advance, of being a future bad debtor; the contrary would be closer to the truth. It is the bad debtor who must be understood as if the marks had not sufficiently 'taken' on him, as if he were or had been unmarked [by the technologies of debt]. He has merely widened, beyond the limits allowed, the gap that separated the voice of alliance and the body of filiation, to such a degree that it is necessary to re-establish the equilibrium through an increase in pain" (191). In another place they add, "Is the instability derived in relation to an ideal of exchange, or is it already given in the preconditions, included in the heterogeneity of the terms that compose the prestations and counter-prestations?" (187).
7. In "What Is Global Literature?" the editors of *World Lite* read *Wizard* as being about the identity of exile or recognizing and retrieving a "forsaken

community" by reinvigorating its language (in connection with a depoliticized poststructuralism). Focusing on debt, however, complicates identity inside instruments of finance, showing how unequal identities are structurally created.

8. As Robert Hullot-Kentor notes in his "Translator's Introduction" to Adorno's *Aesthetic Theory*, "Aesthetic concepts would become the memory of nature sedimented in art, which for Adorno takes shape in *Aesthetic Theory* as the unconscious, mimetically written history of human suffering against which enlightenment elsewhere seals itself off" (xiii). Adorno knew that suffering is also subsumable in the concept and is difficult to disassociate from other topoi, as we recognize it in sentimental, criminal, or victimization narratives, for example. However, for Adorno, there is a part of human suffering that cannot be reduced to its administered, calculable, predictable form.
9. Linked to the money economy, realism, says Fredric Jameson, is identified in "the shift from the diachronic to the synchronic" (*Antinomies* 222), a sense that instead of progressively accumulating experience in time, society would be spread out in "independent tokens of narration" (226) that intersect in chance meetings and momentary exchanges, "interweaving of a host of such lots or fates" (222). In realism, Jameson observes, protagonists are replaced by a slew of secondary characters, tidbits of everyday life, and unnamable feelings that occur simultaneously, thus turning chronological time into geographical space. Realism for Jameson (not a different classification from modernism but rather a different methodology) is thus the outgrowth of the "irreconcilable divorce between lived experience and the intelligible which characterizes modernity" (33), "the radical distinction between naming and representational construction" (35).
10. As Clover is interested in how financialization renders time as space, he is less attentive to how the "Third World" is the particular space where debt replaces the worker for the extrapolation of maximum value. Others have talked about the time of the "Third World" as the time of the Other, where the primitive is used to prove the temporal superiority and domination of Western modernity and its modes of power. As discussed by Johannes Fabian, among others, modern secular science "*spatialized* Time" (15): "Anthropology's efforts to construct relations with its Other by means of temporal devices implied affirmation of differences as *distance*" (16). Anthropological representations of different cultural and ethnic populations coexisting simultaneously yet scientifically categorized as in different historical stages speak to evolutionism or a Newtonian physicalism. Processes of growth and progress, says Fabian, are thereby mapped onto existing geographical terrain: "In the study

of 'unchanging' primitive culture, temporal relations can be disregarded in favor of spatial relations" (18). According to the views that Fabian criticizes, juxtaposed cultural and social examples of prior evolutionary moments coexist in the present so that "the civilized" can actually *see* the signs of modern advancement across space.

11. Mostly focused on Europe, Piketty's analysis of inequality concentrates for the most part on domestic inequalities inside of rich nations, which he sees as of greater consequence than inequalities between such nations. Contrasting his views to David Ricardo's, Piketty maintains that the main cause of inequality is a change in the capital return (inherited wealth: e.g., savings, machinery, housing, real estate, financial assets such as incomes from profits, dividends, rents, interest) / national income (wages, benefits, social supports) ratio within a country. Piketty argues that the income from capital, adjusted for spending levels and including earnings from foreign investments, has been steady in relation to the aggregate of individual earnings, except for in the twentieth century, when capital's share was diminished due to the destruction of the world wars and the Depression. As a consequence, in the time period between the world wars and lingering on until the early seventies, inequality decreased. The twenty-first century, then, is most likely to look more like the nineteenth than the twentieth in terms of inequality levels. Piketty feels comfortable in concluding, "Inequality is not necessarily bad in itself: the key question is to decide whether it is justified, whether there are reasons for it" (19). Partly, this conclusion can be said to emerge from the way Piketty describes inequality as natural within the economy. This means he cannot consider the idea of inequality between specific ethnic, national, or cultural populations or inequality as imposed by some because they hold political and/or economic power over others and can collect from the productivity of others.
12. I thank Peter Hitchcock for pointing out Piketty's statements about literary realism.
13. The two-hundred- to three-hundred-year span that Piketty analyzes might have witnessed vast transformations in how capital accumulation is represented even within European crises, which are Piketty's focus. As Piketty admits, "Clearly, the structure of wealth has been utterly transformed since the time of *Mansfield Park*" (120).
14. "It is not easy to identify capitalists as persons" (Berardi 79)—a person is not the physical counterpart to a sum but rather, he notes, an effect: "Statistics, figures, indexes, fears, and expectations are not linguistic representations of some referent that can be found somewhere in the physical world" (79). These neoliberal rubrics show numbers as positive and real, while their referents

have vanished, thus participating in "the destruction of the existing world" (105).

15. The first step of "dereferentializaton" is the classical Marxist abstraction, which separates the worker's body from the usefulness of the things he makes. In the second phase, information replaces things, and the body is exiled from the field of communication. The third level is neoliberal financial abstraction, where valuation does not even pass through signs or things. "When the referent is cancelled," Berardi writes, "when profit is made possible by the mere circulation of money, the production of cars, books, and bread become [*sic*] superfluous" (104).
16. "There were many theories about the strange illness of the second Ruler of the Free Republic," the opening line runs, "but the most frequent on people's lips were five" (3).
17. The doctors remark on the fear in the Ruler's eyes, "like the eyes of a child stricken with the unexpected and the unknown" (471).
18. *Wizard* has been seen to draw a legacy from Latin American dictator novels. The "literary response in the wake of dictatorship on both continents shares certain important similarities" (Colson 136), including a recourse to parody, a humanization of the dictatorial character, and a demystification of authoritarian power.
19. In large part, in the history of realism, synchronicities are established, says Jameson, through rumor, "which enlarges the facts of interrelationship and transmits them onward to a circulation through the collectivity" (*Antinomies* 228). Rumor runs rampant in *Wizard*, outside of the control of the nation's institutions that spread their own rumors. Colson understands the multiplicity of rumors in *Wizard* as fracturing the Ruler's power, bringing "into relief that the regime's claims to complete control are unfounded" (137) and ending "the Ruler's efforts to arrest time" (138) by pluralizing contributing narrators, each with a different take on the events and the workings of power. Brady Smith agrees that the "multiple voices certainly work against the Ruler and the hegemony toward which he aspires" (178). I find this reading difficult to concur with. As I discuss later on, the hegemony is not weakened by the onslaught of rumors. I, rather, follow Jameson in thinking that the simultaneity of different events in different time registers introduces social conflict.
20. The temporal sequencing, facts surrounding events, and founding mythologies, just as the names of ministers, often change.
21. Critics have interpreted the burgeoning of *petit récits* in the text as challenging the top-down administration of dictatorial rule. Colson, for example, maintains that the Ruler's power hinges on his claims to be able to arrest time—"to

make the past and the present frozen and timeless" (139)—and that the proliferation of narrators, rumors, and storytellers wrests the control of time into independent frames, each presaging the Ruler's "failed attempt to halt the march of time and indefinitely postpone the future on a national scale" (143). Gikandi agrees that "the phantasmal allegory of the dictator who sets out to control time and desire" (164) comes up against "the incompleteness or incommensurability of the narratives that arise out of . . . incomplete journeys and by the series of strategies that the novelist deploys as he tries to encompass fragmentation" (168). Macdonald construes the multiple sources of narration as envisioning an internationalized populism no longer bound to the nation: "The populism the Movement of the Voice of the People advocates," he explains, "stretches beyond continental borders as well as beyond national and ethnic ones," adopting "the diasporic interests and transnational tenor" (62) of Ngugi's political writings. In addition, some critics have noted that the multiple narrators highlight themes of self-construction and performance in the text: Nyawira, for example, "could change itself into any character, sometimes so realistically that even those who thought they knew her well because of seeing her on platforms in many student political events were often unable to say whether it was really Nyawira on the stage" (80). Smith observes that "the text of the novel . . . is presented throughout as a kind of oral performance" (177). McLaren proposes that *Wizard* "suggests a writing method akin to the way jazz artists develop their solos through reinventing the melodies over recurring choruses" (153). John Updike adds that readers "would do well to remember that [*Wizard*] is a translation from a language whose narrative traditions are mostly oral and heavy on performance." He cites Ngugi saying of the book, "The characters are engaged in the constant performance of their own being for the narrative. You never quite know who they are. Often they reinvent themselves through performance." As Colson concludes, "The satirical-allegorical distance created by the world of *Wizard of the Crow* serves to heighten the actual critique of authoritarian government because it brings into relief that the regime's claims to complete control are unfounded. The tenuous position of the dictator underlies all his acts of violence and performances of power" (137). There is no doubt that performance and orality are predominant themes in the text that lend themselves to interpreting the text in terms of postcolonial identity construction. Yet such readings also marginalize what I think is the more original contribution that *Wizard* makes to literature by teasing out a narrative structure particular to debt.

22. Tajirika—known now as the Emperor Titus Flavius Vespasianus Whitehead—takes control of the armed forces in order to implement "a new

era of imperial democracy" with the "construction of a modern coliseum on the site once earmarked for Marching to Heaven" (754), the "TALLEST BUILDING IN AFRICA; A REAL MARCHING TO HEAVEN" (762) now under the auspices of the Global Insurance Corporation.

23. A. G. fails in his police job and leaves in response to a car accident, which he interprets as a divine sign. After a women's protest at the gates of Paradise, where the Marching to Heaven tower is planned to be built, A. G. chases the wizard and Nyawira, who are dressed as beggars that keep changing shape and location, when he comes across a sign warning "TOUCH THIS HOUSE AT YOUR PERIL" (77) and turns back. Later he returns to get treatment from the wizard. He tells the wizard that he is sure he has enemies who are causing him not to get a promotion at work. Though he does not know the identity of his enemy, the wizard tells him to check the accident reports involving *matatus* (privately owned minibuses used for communal commuting in Kenya), and he will see there that his enemy has been fatally injured. Sure enough, an accident happens killing fifteen people. Convinced that his enemy has been sacrificed in the accident, A. G. quits his job and becomes a wandering storyteller.
24. The symptoms include an inability to look away from the mirror while scratching his skin and occasionally jumping in the bathtub. His response when confronted is as though "his mind [were] in another world and distrustful of the one he now inhabited" (172). The loss of language is later diagnosed by the wizard as "white ache," a depression caused by his inability to turn white no matter how wealthy he became.
25. Berardi sees this transformation of language away from signification as a result of language learning no longer being the reproductive and affective duty of solely the mother but increasingly the effect of informational and media technologies: "The separation of language learning from the body of the mother and from the body in general is changing language itself, and is changing the relation between the body and language" (101).
26. Balogun writes, "Soyinka's evolution from a nationalist writer espousing the bourgeois philosophy of 'pure art' into a committed writer inspired by socialist ideals occurred in the second half of the 1960s and was generously commented upon by liberal and radical critics alike" (507).
27. Impersonating the Professor mockingly, Samson imitates postcolonial power by spewing petty insults on Salubi, joking that his physical depravity, his farting and bad breath, make him most suitable for promotion. "One of these days," says Salubi, "I will find out where he hides the money" (164), but he never does. "Go on, you are sacked" (158), returns Samson. The postcolonial state is thus mocked as an absurd imitation of production's promise.

28. "For Soyinka Western science constricts and compartmentalizes reality whereas 'African metaphysics' sees no contradiction between modern technology and the gods" (Hunt 78).
29. The connection between capital and death monsters was noted by Marx. The new forms the death monsters have taken in finance culture have been analyzed by critics. See, for example, not only Annie McClanahan's analysis of the horror film (143–83) but also Fred Botting: "Zombie debt is a debt that will not die, that cannot be repaid; it signals an almost total absorption into a world financial market carrying on without thought or concern for anything other than accumulation. Hence the horror: one can neither kill nor escape the global network that circumscribes planetary existence and the zombie effects of producing so many debt-bound automatons."
30. As K. J. Phillips remarks, "Soyinka criticizes the Faustian drive in order to exorcise the Western Faustus from Africa. But then, surprisingly, he salvages a portion of that drive by insisting it has always characterized his favorite god of the Yoruba pantheon, Ogun" (140), the god of death and taxi drivers.
31. Soyinka's interpretation of the god Ogun, of death and taxi drivers, is more complicated than my own metaphoric use. I am taking Ogun to represent the source of indebtedness, in some ways linked to economies of imperialism and dead capital. On the other hand, Soyinka admires Ogun for his status as a god who became embodied, descended to the human world, and was engaged in human interactions:

    > He came down decked in palm fronds and was crowned king. In war after war he led his men to victory. Then, . . . the trickster god left a gourd of palm wine for the thirsty deity. Ogun found it exceptionally delicious and drained the gourd to the dregs . . . Ogun is the embodiment of challenge, the Promethean instinct in man, constantly at the service of society for its full self-realisation . . . Ogun's action did not take place in a vacuum. His venture was necessarily a drama of individual stress, yet even his moment of individuation was communicant, one which enabled the other gods to share, whose end-in-view was no less than a strengthening of the communal psyche. (*Myth* 29–30)

    Here one hears echoes not only of Jesus and obviously Prometheus but also, perhaps more fundamentally, of Zarathustra. For Soyinka, Ogun is not only between the spiritual and the physical, not only between gods and humans, but also a type of cultural bridge, a sign of the complementary that exists between mythologies and cultures, where each culture is unique and also possesses shared features with "a common humanity" (*Myth* xii).

32. Berardi observes, "Finance is an effect of the virtualization of reality, acting on the psycho-cognitive sphere of the economy. But at the same time, finance is an effect of the deterritorialization of wealth . . . Finance is the transversal function of immaterialization, and the performative action of indexicality. Statistics, figures, indexes, fears, and expectations are not linguistic representations of some economic referent that can be found somewhere in the physical world, signifiers referring to a signified" (79).
33. Whitefish Energy is located in the hometown of Secretary of the Interior Ryan Zinke. The head of the private equity firm that backs Whitefish, Joe Colonnetta, was a major donor to Donald Trump's presidential campaign.
34. As vice mayor of San Juan Rafael Jaume reports on *Democracy Now!*, "FEMA's statement of this morning says clearly, 'The decision to award a contract to Whitefish Energy was made exclusively by Puerto Rico Electric Power Authority, PREPA. FEMA was not involved in the selection. Questions regarding the awarding of this contract should be directed to PREPA.' The following says, 'Any language in any contract between PREPA and Whitefish that states FEMA approved that contract is inaccurate.' Strong words." Meanwhile, he says, Article 68 of the contract specifies, "'By executing this contract, PREPA hereby represents and warrants that FEMA has reviewed and approved of this contract and confirmed that the contract is an acceptable form to qualify for funding from FEMA and other U.S. government agencies.' Totally the opposite in contrast to what FEMA is saying" (Goodman and González).
35. Nevertheless, Yeampierre and Klein witness efforts on the part of Puerto Ricans to use the resources of the community to build back up the infrastructure in sustainable ways. With the assistance of Puerto Ricans living on the US mainland, Puerto Ricans are avoiding helplessness provoked by the devastation of the power grid by distributing and sharing solar-powered generators and reviving local agriculture. It is too early to tell where such efforts will lead.

# Works Cited


Adorno, Theodor. *Aesthetic Theory*. Eds. Gretel Adorno and Rolf Tiedemann. Trans. Robert Hullot-Kentor. Minneapolis: University of Minnesota Press, 1997.

Amin, Samir. *Capitalism in the Age of Globalization: The Management of Contemporary Society*. London: Zed Books, 1997.

Appadurai, Arjun. *Banking On Words: The Failure of Language in the Age of Derivative Finance*. Chicago: University of Chicago Press, 2016.

Aronoff, Kate. "Armed Federal Agents Enter Warehouse in Puerto Rico to Seize Hoarded Electrical Equipment." *The Intercept* (10 Jan. 2018): https://theintercept.com/2018/01/10/puerto-rico-electricity-prepa-hurricane-maria/. Accessed 12 Jan. 2018.

Aronoff, Kate. "Puerto Rico Is On Track for Historic Debt Forgiveness—Unless Wall Street Gets Its Way." *The Intercept* (4 Oct. 2017): https://theintercept.com/2017/10/04/puerto-rico-debt-forgiveness-hurricane-maria/. Accessed 25 Oct. 2017.

Arrighi, Giovanni. *The Long Twentieth Century: Money, Power, and the Origins of Our Times*. London: Verso, 1994.

Ascher, Ivan. *Portfolio Society: On the Capitalist Mode of Prediction*. New York: Zone Books, 2016.

Bagehot, Walter. *Lombard Street: A Description of the Money Market*. 8th ed. London: Kegan Paul, Trench, & Co., 1882.

Bakhtin, M. M. *The Dialogic Imagination: Four Essays*. Ed. Michael Holquist. Trans. Caryl Emerson and Michael Holquist. Austin: University of Texas Press, 1981.

Balogun, F. Odun. "Wole Soyinka and the Literary Aesthetic of African Socialism." *Black Literature Forum* 22, 3 (Autumn 1988): 503–30.

Baucom, Ian. *Spectres of the Atlantic: Finance Capital, Slavery, and the Philosophy of History*. Durham, NC: Duke University Press, 2005.

Baudrillard, Jean. *The Consumer Society: Myths and Structures*. London: Sage, 1998.

Bauman, Zygmunt. *Wasted Lives: Modernity and Its Outcasts*. Cambridge: Polity, 2004.

Beckman, Ericka. *Capital Fictions: The Literature of Latin America's Export Age*. Minneapolis: University of Minnesota Press, 2013.

Berardi, Franco. "Bifo." In *The Uprising: On Poetry and Finance*. Cambridge, MA: Semiotext(e), 2012.

Blanchard, Sidney Laman. "A Biography of a Bad Shilling." *Household Words* 2 (Jan. 1851): 420–26.

Botting, Fred. "Undead-Ends: Zombie Debt/Zombie Theory." *Postmodern Culture* 23, 3 (May 2013): https://muse.jhu.edu/article/554618.

Bowen, H. V. *The Business of Empire: The East India Company and Imperial Britain*. Cambridge: Cambridge University Press, 2008.

Brantlinger, Patrick. *Fictions of State: Culture and Credit in Britain, 1694–1994*. Ithaca, NY: Cornell University Press, 1996.

Cleary, Joe. "Realism after Modernism and the Literary World System." *Modern Language Quarterly* 73, 3 (Sept. 2012): 255–68.

Clover, Joshua. "Autumn of the System: Poetry and Financial Capital." *Journal of Narrative Theory* 41, 1 (Spring 2011): 34–52.

Clover, Joshua. "Value/Theory/Crisis." *PMLA* 127, 1 (Jan. 2012): 107–14.

Colson, Robert L. "Arresting Time, Resisting Arrest: Narrative Time and the African Dictator in Ngugi wa Thiong'o's *Wizard of the Crow*." *Research in African Literatures* 42, 1 (Spring 2011): 133–53.

Dayen, David. "Jamie Dimon and Other People's Money: How JPMorgan Chase Paid Its Fine for the 2008 Mortgage Crisis—with Phony Mortgages!" *The Nation* (23 Oct. 2017): 12–15 and 20.

Deleuze, Gilles, and Félix Guattari. *Anti-Oedipus*. Trans. Robert Hurley, Mark Seem, and Helen R. Lane. Minneapolis: University of Minnesota Press, 1983.

Denis, Nelson. "Orwell in Puerto Rico: Congress 'Promises' a New Dictatorship." *The Nation* (15 Apr. 2016): https://www.thenation.com/article/orwell-in-puerto-rico-congress-promises-a-new-dictatorship/. Accessed 23 Aug. 2018.

Derrida, Jacques. *Given Time: I. Counterfeit Money*. Trans. Peggy Kamuf. Chicago: University of Chicago Press, 1992.

Dickens, Charles. *Dombey and Son*. Ed. Alan Horsman. Oxford: Oxford University Press, 1974.

Editors. "What Is Global Literature?" *World Lite* 17 (Fall 2013): https://nplusonemag.com/issue-17/the-intellectual-situation/world-lite/. Accessed 14 Aug. 2017.

Fabian, Johannes. *Time and the Other: How Anthropology Makes Its Object*. New York: Columbia University Press, 1983.
Feuser, Willfried F. "Wole Soyinka: The Problem of Authenticity." *Black American Literature Forum* 22, 3 (Autumn 1988): 555–75.
Friedman, Zack. "Student Loan Debt in 2017: A $1.3 Trillion Crisis." *Forbes* (21 Feb. 2017): https://www.forbes.com/sites/zackfriedman/2017/02/21/student-loan-debt-statistics-2017/#f332fc5dabab. Accessed 8 Jan. 2018.
Ghosh, Amitav. *Sea of Poppies*. New York: Farrar, Straus and Giroux, 2008.
Gikandi, Simon. "The Postcolonial Wizard." *Transition* 98 (2008): 156–69.
González, Juan. "Juan González on How Puerto Rico's Economic 'Death Spiral' Is Tied to Legacy of Colonialism." *Democracy Now!* (26 Nov. 2015): https://www.democracynow.org/2015/11/26/juan_gonzalez_on_how_puerto_ricos?utm_source=Democracy+Now!&utm_campaign=8e049bc5cf-Daily_Digest&utm_medium=email&utm_term=0_fa2346a853-8e049bc5cf-190579529. Accessed 19 Apr. 2017.
Goodlad, Lauren M. E. *The Victorian Geopolitical Aesthetic: Realism, Sovereignty, and Transnational Experience*. Oxford: Oxford University Press, 2015.
Goodman, Amy, and Juan González. "Mayor Carmen Yulín Cruz Condemns 'Indefensible' Whitefish Contract and Calls for PREPA Chief's Firing." *Democracy Now!* (31 Oct. 2017): https://www.democracynow.org/2017/10/31/mayor_carmen_yulin_cruz_condemns_indefensible. Accessed 2 Nov. 2017.
Graeber, David. *Debt: The First 5,000 Years*. Brooklyn, NY: Melville House, 2011, 2012, 2014.
Greiner, Rae. *Sympathetic Realism in Nineteenth-Century British Fiction*. Baltimore, MD: Johns Hopkins University Press, 2012.
Hamid, Mohsin. *How to Get Filthy Rich in Rising Asia*. New York: Riverhead Books, 2013.
Harvey, David. *A Brief History of Neoliberalism*. Oxford: Oxford University Press, 2005.
Hernández, Arelis R., and Laurie McGinley. "Harvard Study Estimates That Thousands Died in Puerto Rico Due to Hurricane Maria." *Washington Post* (29 May 2018): https://www.washingtonpost.com/national/harvard-study-estimates-thousands-died-in-puerto-rico-due-to-hurricane-maria/2018/05/29/1a82503a-6070-11e8-a4a4-c070ef53f315_story.html?utm_term=.fadaa26e71e2&wpisrc=al_news__alert-national&wpmk=1. Accessed 29 May 2018.
Hudson, Peter James. *Bankers and Empire: How Wall Street Colonized the Caribbean*. Chicago: University of Chicago Press, 2017.
Hughes, Langston. "White Shadows in a Black Land." *Crisis* 39 (May 1932): 157.

Hullot-Kentor, Robert. "Translator's Introduction." In *Aesthetic Theory*. By Theodor Adorno. Eds. Gretel Adorno and Rolf Tiedemann. Trans. Robert Hullot-Kentor. Minneapolis: University of Minnesota Press, 1997. Pp. xi–xxi.

Hunt, Geoffrey. "Two African Aesthetics: Soyinka vs. Cabral." In *Marxism and African Literature*. Ed. Georg M. Gugelberger. London: Currey, 1985. Pp. 64–93.

Ingham, Geoffrey. *The Nature of Money*. Cambridge: Polity, 2004.

Jaffe, Audrey. *The Affective Life of the Average Man: The Victorian Novel and the Stock-Market Graph*. Columbus: Ohio State University Press, 2010.

James, Deborah. *Money from Nothing: Indebtedness and Aspiration in South Africa*. Stanford, CA: Stanford University Press, 2015.

Jameson, Fredric. *The Antinomies of Realism*. London: Verso, 2013, 2015.

Jameson, Fredric. *Postmodernism, or The Cultural Logic of Late Capitalism*. Durham, NC: Duke University Press, 1991.

Jeyifro, Biodun. *The Truthful Lie: Essays in a Sociology of African Drama*. London: New Beacon, 1985.

Johnson, James Weldon. *Self-Determining Haiti: Four Articles Reprinted from* The Nation *Embodying a Report of an Investigation Made for the National Association for the Advancement of Colored People*. New York: The Nation, 1920.

Kant, Immanuel. *Critique of the Power of Judgment*. Ed. Paul Guyer. Trans. Paul Guyer and Eric Matthews. Cambridge: Cambridge University Press, 2000.

Kendrick, Walter M. "The Eustace Diamonds: The Truth of Trollope's Fiction." *ELH* 46, 1 (Spring 1979): 136–57.

Kishore, Nishant, et al. "Mortality in Puerto Rico after Hurricane Maria." *New England Journal of Medicine* (29 May 2018): https://www.nejm.org/doi/full/10.1056/NEJMsa1803972?query=featured_home. Accessed 29 May 2018.

Kornbluh, Anna. "Realism's Empire." *Novel* 501, 14 (2017): 150–54.

Kornbluh, Anna. *Realizing Capital: Financial and Psychic Economies in Victorian Form*. New York: Fordham University Press, 2014.

Lanchester, John. *I.O.U.: Why Everyone Owes Everyone and No One Can Pay*. New York: Simon & Schuster, 2010.

Lazzarato, Maurizio. *Governing by Debt*. Trans. Joshua David Jordan. South Pasadena, CA: Semiotext(e), 2015.

Lazzarato, Maurizio. *The Making of Indebted Man: An Essay on the Neoliberal Condition*. Trans. Joshua David Jordan. Los Angeles, CA: Semiotext(e), 2012.

Lukacs, Gyorgy. "Realism in the Balance." In *The Norton Anthology of Theory and Criticism*. 1st ed. Eds. Vincent B. Leitch, William E. Cain, Laurie A. Finke, Barbara E. Johnson, John McGowan, and Jeffrey J. Williams. New York: W. W. Norton, 2001. Pp. 1030–58.

Lynch, Deidre Shauna. *The Economy of Character: Novels, Market Culture, and the Business of Inner Meaning*. Chicago: University of Chicago Press, 1998.

Macdonald, Ian P. "The Cybogre Manifesto: Time, Utopia, and Globality in Ngugi's *Wizard of the Crow*." *Research in African Literatures* 47, 1 (Spring 2016): 57–75.

Markovits, Stefanie. "Form Things: Looking at Genre through Victorian Diamonds." *Victorian Studies* 52, 4 (Summer 2010): 591–619.

Marlowe, Christopher. *The Tragical History of Doctor Faustus*. Ed. Alexander Dyce. Newgate: John Wright, 1616.

Marx, Karl. *Capital: A Critique of Political Economy*. Vol. 1. Ed. Frederick Engels. Trans. Samuel Moore and Edward Aveling. New York: International Publishers, 1967.

Marx, Karl. "Comments on James Mill, *Eléments D'économie Politique*." *Marxists.org*. https://www.marxists.org/archive/marx/works/1844/james-mill/. Accessed 24 Apr. 2017.

McClanahan, Annie. "Dead Pledges: Debt, Horror, and the Credit Crisis." *Post45* (5 July 2012): http://post45.research.yale.edu/2012/05/dead-pledges-debt-horror-and-the-credit-crisis/. Accessed 9 Jan. 2017.

McLaren, Joseph. "From the National to the Global: Satirical Magic Realism in Ngugi's 'Wizard of the Crow.'" *The Global South* 2, 2 (Fall 2008): 150–58.

McPhee, Martha. *Dear Money*. Boston: Houghton Mifflin Harcourt, 2010.

Michie, Elsie B. *The Vulgar Question of Money: Heiresses, Materialism, and the Novel of Manners from Jane Austen to Henry James*. Baltimore, MD: Johns Hopkins University Press, 2011.

Miller, Andrew H. *Novels behind Glass: Commodity Culture and Victorian Narrative*. Cambridge: Cambridge University Press, 1995.

Morales, Ed. "Who Is Responsible for Puerto Rico's Debt?" *The Nation* (7 June 2016): https://www.thenation.com/article/who-is-responsible-for-puerto-ricos-debt/. Accessed 8 July 2017.

Negri, Antonio. *Marx beyond Marx: Lessons on the* Grundrisse. Ed. Jim Fleming. Trans. Harry Cleaver, Michael Ryan, and Maurizio Viano. Brooklyn, NY: Autonomedia, 1991.

Nelson, Denis. "Orwell in Puerto Rico: Congress 'Promises' a New Dictatorship." *The Nation* (15 Apr. 2016): https://www.thenation.com/article/orwell-in-puerto-rico-congress-promises-a-new-dictatorship/. Accessed 6 July 2017.

Ngugi wa Thiong'o. *Globalectics: Theory and the Politics of Knowing*. New York: Columbia University Press, 2012.

Ngugi wa Thiong'o. *Wizard of the Crow*. Trans. Ngugi wa Thiong'o. New York: Anchor Books, 2006.

Nietzsche, Friedrich. "Second Essay: 'Guilt,' 'Bad Conscience,' and the Like." In *On the Genealogy of Morals and Ecce Homo*. Ed. and trans. Walter Kaufman. New York: Vintage Books, 1967.

Nilges, Mathias. "Finance Capital and the Time of the Novel or, Money without Narrative Qualities." *Topia: Canadian Journal of Cultural Studies* 30–31 (Fall 2013 / Spring 2014): 31–46.

Nunokawa, Jeff. *The Afterlife of Property: Domestic Security and the Victorian Novel*. Princeton, NJ: Princeton University Press, 1994.

Okpara, Enoch E. "The Rôle of Touts in Passenger Transport in Nigeria." *Journal of Modern African Studies* 26, 2 (1988): 327–35.

Oliphant, Laurence. "The Autobiography of a Joint-Stock Company (Limited)." *Blackwood's Edinburgh Magazine* 120 (July 1876): 96–122.

Phillips, K. J. "Exorcising Faustus from Africa: Wole Soyinka's 'The Road.'" *Comparative Literature Studies* 27, 2 (1990): 140–57.

Piketty, Thomas. *Capital in the Twenty-First Century*. Trans. Arthur Goldhammer. Cambridge, MA: Harvard University Press, 2014.

Plotz, John. "Discreet Jewels: Victorian Diamond Narratives and the Problem of Sentimental Value." In *The Secret Life of Things: Animals, Objects, and It-Narratives in Eighteenth-Century England*. Ed. Mark Blackwell. Lewisburg, PA: Bucknell University Press, 2007. Pp. 329–54.

Poovey, Mary. *Genres of the Credit Economy: Mediating Value in Eighteenth- and Nineteenth Century-Britain*. Chicago: University of Chicago Press, 2008.

Poovey, Mary. *A History of the Modern Fact: Problems of Knowledge in the Sciences of Wealth and Society*. Chicago: University of Chicago Press, 1998.

Psomiades, Kathy Alexis. "Heterosexual Exchange and Other Victorian Fictions: 'The Eustace Diamonds' and Victorian Anthropology." *Novel* 33, 1 (Autumn 1999): 93–118.

Rae, George. "The Testimony of a Balance Sheet." In *The Country Banker, His Clients, Cares, and Work from an Experience of Forty Years*. 1885; rev. ed. London: John Murray, 1930. Pp. 14–26.

Reed, John R. "A Friend to Mammon: Speculation in Victorian Literature." *Victorian Studies* 27, 2 (Winter 1984): 179–202.

Ross, Stephen. "Speculative Modernism." In *Reconnecting Aestheticism and Modernism: Continuities, Revisions, Speculations*. Eds. Bénédicte Coste, Catherine Delyfer, and Christine Reynier. New York: Routledge, 2017. Pp. 139–53.

Roth, Alan. "He Thought He Was Right (but Wasn't): Property Law in Anthony Trollope's 'The Eustace Diamonds.'" *Stanford Law Review* 44, 4 (Apr. 1992): 879–97.

Scahill, Jeremy, and David Harvey. "Leading Marxist Scholar David Harvey on Trump, Wall Street, and Debt Peonage." *The Intercept* (21 Jan. 2018): https://theintercept.com/2018/01/21/marxist-scholar-david-harvey-on-trump-wall-street-and-debt-peonage/. Accessed 9 May 2018.

Sennett, Richard. *The Fall of Public Man*. New York: Alfred A. Knopf, 1977.

Sharpe, Jenny. *Allegories of Empire: The Figure of Woman in the Colonial Text*. Minneapolis: University of Minnesota Press, 1993.

Shohat, Ella. "Notes on the 'Post-colonial.'" *Social Text* 31/32 (1992): 99–113.

Shonkwiler, Alison. *The Financial Imaginary: Economic Mystification and the Limits of Realist Fiction*. Minneapolis: University of Minnesota Press, 2017.

Sidgwick, Henry. "What Is Money?" *Fortnightly Review* 31, 5 (Apr. 1879): 563–75.

Silver-Greenberg, Jessica, and Stacy Cowley. "A Boom in Credit Cards: Great News for Banks, Less So Consumers." *New York Times* (19 Oct. 2017): https://www.nytimes.com/2017/10/19/business/credit-cards-debt-banks.html. Accessed 20 Oct. 2017.

Smith, Brady. "Wizards, Superwonders, and a Fictional African State: Money and the Ecology of the Grotesque in Ngugi wa Thiong'o's *Wizard of the Crow*." *Research in African Literatures* 46, 3 (2015): 165–89.

Sorkin, Andrew Ross. "DealBook Briefing: JPMorgan Shows Wall Street Is Still Hurting." *New York Times* (12 Jan. 2018). Accessed 12 Jan. 2018.

Soyinka, Wole. *Collected Plays I*. Oxford: Oxford University Press, 1973.

Soyinka, Wole. *Myth, Literature and the African World*. London: Cambridge University Press, 1976.

Soyinka, Wole. "The Writer in an African State." *Transition* 75/76 (1997): 350–56.

Sutherland, John. "Introduction." Rev. In *The Eustace Diamonds*. By Anthony Trollope. New York: Penguin, 2004. Pp. 7–27.

Torruella, Juan R. *The Supreme Court and Puerto Rico: The Doctrine of Separate but Unequal*. Río Piedras: Editorial de la Universidad de Puerto Rico, 1985.

Trollope, Anthony. *The Eustace Diamonds*. Rev. ed. New York: Penguin Classics, 2004.

Trollope, Anthony. *The Last Chronicle of Barset*. New York: Penguin Classics, 2002.

Trollope, Anthony. *Phineas Finn: The Irish Member. In Two Volumes*. Vol. 1. London: Oxford University Press, 1937.

Trollope, Anthony. *The Way We Live Now*. New York: Barnes & Noble Classics, 2005.

Updike, John. "Extended Performance: Saving the Republic of Aburiria." *New Yorker* (31 July 2006): http://www.newyorker.com/magazine/2006/07/31/extended-performance. Accessed 26 July 2017.

Walsh, Mary Williams. "Puerto Rico: A Debt Problem That Kept Boiling Over." *New York Times* (5 May 2017): https://www.nytimes.com/2017/05/05/business/dealbook/puerto-rico-debt.html. Accessed 6 May 2017.

Walter, Jess. *The Financial Lives of the Poets*. New York: Harper Perennial, 2009.

Wortham, Simon Morgan. "What We Owe to Retroactivity: The Origin and Future of Debt." *Postmodern Culture* 23, 3 (May 2013): http://muse.jhu.edu.proxy.lib.fsu.edu/article/554615.

Yeampierre, Elizabeth, and Naomi Klein. "Imagine a Puerto Rico Recovery Designed by Puerto Ricans." *The Intercept* (20 Oct. 2017): https://theintercept.com/2017/10/20/puerto-rico-hurricane-debt-relief/. Accessed 25 Oct. 2017.

CPSIA information can be obtained
at www.ICGtesting.com
Printed in the USA
BVHW09s2130231018
531024BV00009B/118/P